HISTORIC SCOTLAND

PILGRIMAGE IN
MEDIEVAL SCOTLAND

Ian
with all good wishes

Peter Yeoman

For my father William Alexander Yeoman
and in memory of my mother Dora Wetherell Yeoman

HISTORIC SCOTLAND

PILGRIMAGE IN MEDIEVAL SCOTLAND

PETER YEOMAN

B. T. Batsford Ltd / Historic Scotland

First published 1999

Typeset by Bernard Cavender Design & Greenwood Graphics Publishing
and printed by WBC Book Manufacturers

Published by B. T. Batsford Ltd
583 Fulham Road, London SW6 5BY

A CIP catalogue record for this book is
available from the British Library.

ISBN 0 7134 8174 9 (limp)

(Front cover) Detail from the tomb of Alexander Macleod (d. 1546), St Clement's Church, Rodel, Harris.
(Back cover) Laggangairn standing stones, on the pilgrimage route to Whithorn, Galloway, incised with crosses by early pilgrims.

Contents

List of illustrations   6

List of colour plates   8

Acknowledgements   9

Foreword   10

1   To be a pilgrim   11

2   Saints and shrines in Strathclyde   16

3   St Ninian of Whithorn, and the shrines around Edinburgh and the Borders   33

4   Fife: the pilgrims' kingdom   53

5   St Columba of Iona, and the shrines of Perthshire   75

6   St Magnus and the Orkney shrines   93

7   James IV: Scotland's pilgrim king   101

8   Scots pilgrimage abroad   110

Pilgrimage places to visit   121

Further reading   124

Index   125

Illustrations

1 Principal pilgrimage places 12
2 A medieval pilgrim 13
3 Tomb-shrine of Edward the Confessor 14
4 East end of Glasgow Cathedral 17
5 Sketch plan and section of east end of Glasgow Cathedral 20
6 Later thirteenth-century Chapter Seal, Glasgow Cathedral 21
7 Pilgrims at the shrine of St Kentigern behind the high altar, Glasgow Cathedral 22
8 Pilgrims at the tomb-shrine in the lower church, Glasgow Cathedral 23
9 South aisle passage and stairs down to the under church, Glasgow Cathedral 24
10 Site of St Kentigern's tomb, Glasgow Cathedral 25
11 Glasgow Cathedral with Bishop's Castle, manses and almhouses 26
12 Reconstructed arcading, Glasgow Cathedral 28
13 Govan sarcophagus 28
14 Plan of St Miren's Abbey, Paisley 30
15 St Miren's Aisle, Paisley 31
16 Scenes from the life of St Miren, Paisley 32
17 Manuscript illumination of St Ninian 34
18 Northumbrian minster at Whithorn, late eighth century 37
19 Whithorn – later medieval cathedral plan 38
20 Whithorn – cut-away of east end shrine and crypt 40
21 Whithorn – ambulatory routes 41
22 Whithorn – oak statue of St Ninian(?) 42
23 Whithorn – late medieval barrel-vaulted crypt 43

24 St Ninian's Cave 43
25 Whithorn Priory reconstruction c 1500 44
26 Melrose Abbey 45
27 Melrose Abbey – possible fragments of St Waltheof's tomb-shrine 47
28 Melrose Abbey – reconstruction of the tomb-shrine 47
29 Badge mould from Dundrennan Abbey, and badges from Whithorn, Melrose and Fast Castle 48
30 Crosskirk, Peebles – reconstruction drawing 49
31 Bass Rock – St Baldred's chapel 50
32 St Triduana's Chapel – engraving of the interior 52
33 St Andrews' sarcophagus 54
34 St Mary's, Chichester – interior of a medieval hospital 56
35 Map of Fife pilgrimage routes 57
36 Pilgrims' road in north-west Fife 58
37 Guardbridge – crossing the Eden, west of St Andrews 59
38 North Berwick harbour 60
39 St Andrews' pilgrims' badges and badge moulds 61
40 Isle of May – translation of the relics in the ninth century 62
41 Isle of May – Santiago pilgrim burial 63
42 St Andrews Cathedral – plan 65
43 St Andrews – Pends gatehouse 66
44 St Andrews – reconstruction of the late medieval shrine chapel 67
45 St Andrew – statue 68
46 St Andrews – reconstruction of the precinct

    in the early sixteenth century 69
47 Dunfermline – interior of the nave 70
48 Dunfermline – thirteenth-century
    enlargement of east end 71
49 Dunfermline – St Margaret's shrine 72
50 Dunfermline – ground plan 73
51 Dunfermline – St Margaret's head shrine 74
52 Dunfermline – thirteenth-century seal 74
53 Iona – island map 76
54 Iona – nineteenth-century impression of
    Columba's monastery 77
55 Iona – plan of sites around the abbey 78
56 Iona – reconstruction of a corner-post
    shrine 80
57 Iona – pilgrims' foot-bath 81
58 Iona – development of the Benedictine
    abbey 82
59 Iona – north transept altar stances 83
60 Iona – early thirteenth-century east end
    plan, access to the undercroft 83
61 Iona – two-storey east end details 84
62 Tomb of Alexander Macleod,
    St Clement's, Rodel 85
63 Dunkeld – Apostles Stone 86
64 Dunkeld – thirteenth-century Chapter Seal 86
65 Kilmichael Glassary bell-shrine 87
66 Guthrie bell-shrine 88
67 *Cathach* of St Columba 89
68 St Fillan's bell 90
69 Shrine of St Patrick's hand 91
70 Grave slab from St Fillan's priory 92
71 St Magnus' Cathedral, Kirkwall 93
72 St Magnus' Cathedral, Kirkwall – statue of
    the saint 94
73 St Magnus' Cathedral, Kirkwall – sketch
    plan of original east end and shrine 95

74 St Magnus' Cathedral, Kirkwall – plan of
    completed church 96
75 St Magnus' Cathedral, Kirkwall – crucifix
    badge mould 97
76 St Magnus', Egilsay 98
77 St Magnus' Cathedral, Kirkwall – south
    choir pier where Magnus' relics were found 98
78 Relics of St Magnus 99
79 St Tredwell's Chapel, Papa Westray 100
80 James IV pilgrimage routes 102
81 Glenluce Priory 104
82 St Duthac's, Tain – twelfth- and fifteenth-
    century reliquary churches 107
83 St Duthac's, Tain – east end of the
    fifteenth-century church 108
84 Principal foreign shrines visited by Scots 111
85 St Cuthbert's Cathedral, Durham 112
86 Christ Church Cathedral, Canterbury 113
87 St William of Perth 114
88 Scots hospice of Santa Andrea delle Fratte,
    Rome 117
89 Pilgrims' badges and *ampullae* from
    Walsingham and Canterbury 118
90 Santiago scallop shell badges 118
91 *Ampullae* and badges from other foreign
    shrines 119
92 Contemporary pilgrimage from Whitekirk
    to St Mary's, Haddington 120

Colour plates

(Between pages 64 and 65)

1 St Ninian(?) on the Whithorn crozier
2 Old Melrose – site of the early Christian monastery
3 St Andrews – the churches and precinct from the air
4 St Andrews – pilgrims arriving from the south
5 St Andrews – streets converging on the cathedral
6 St Margaret, from a fifteenth-century prayer-book

7 Dunfermline – translation of St Margaret 1250
8 Dunfermline – pilgrims in the thirteenth-century shrine chapel
9 Iona – Benedictine abbey with Street of the Dead, Tòrr an Aba, and high crosses in front of Columba's shrine
10 Monymusk Reliquary
11 St Fillan's crozier
12 James IV accompanied by St James the Greater from his *Book of Hours*

Acknowledgements

I am very grateful to all my friends and colleagues who have helped me research this book, especially Simon Taylor of the St Andrews University Scottish Studies Institute, and Richard Fawcett of Historic Scotland. I have also benefited from the guidance of Professor Archie Duncan, Professor Geoffrey Barrow, Mike King of Fife Council Museums, Mark Hall of Perth and Kinross Museums, Derek Hall of the Scottish Urban Archaeological Trust, Estelle Quick of Tain and District Museums, Jerry O' Sullivan and Stephen Driscoll of Glasgow University Archaeological Research Division, Tom Clancy of Department of Celtic, University of Glasgow, Gordon Ewart of Kirkdale Archaeology, Chris Lowe of Headland Archaeology, Ann Brundle of Orkney Museums, and Raymond Lamb. Many of the other Council Archaeologists, notably Lorna Main of Stirling Council, provided me with data from their sites and monuments records, for which I am most grateful. I am pleased to acknowledge the skills of Heather James and all who worked with us on the Isle of May excavations, the results of which prompted me to take up the pilgrim's staff. Once on the path, I received much invaluable direction from the scholarship of the late Monsignor David McRoberts, via the pages of *The Innes Review*. The research was eased by the efforts of the staff of the Scottish Library in Edinburgh City Libraries, who found everything I ever wanted. The invaluable help of the staff of the Royal Commission on the Ancient and Historical Monuments of Scotland is here acknowledged, especially that received from Ian Fisher, Ian Fraser, and Kevin Maclaren. The talents of David Simon, Marion O'Neil and Alan Braby have produced many of the drawings which grace this book. Similarly, I am grateful to the Historic Scotland photographers, Mike Brooks and Chris Hutchison, and especially David Henrie, for their marvellous images, and to Joseph White the photo librarian. Other excellent images were kindly supplied by: Cormac Bourke of the Ulster Museum; Niall M. Robertson; Daphne Brooke; R.M. Crawford, and Tom E. Gray. I am also pleased to offer my thanks to David Caldwell and Jackie Moran of the National Museums of Scotland for helping me to understand and illustrate the artefacts of pilgrimage.

Much of the fieldwork and research was completed during a leave of absence which was kindly granted by Fife Council, and I am grateful to David Rae, Head of Planning, and to Rob Terwey and Neil Gateley for arranging this. I am especially grateful to Sarah Govan for filling the gap so expertly while I was away. The leave of absence was enabled by grants provided by the Russell Trust and the Hunter Archaeological Trust, to whom I offer my sincere thanks. The generous support I received from Ramsay McWhirter made it possible for this book to be completed in the twentieth century. I am indebted to Richard Fawcett, Chris Tabraham, Sally Foster, Olly Owen and David Breeze of Historic Scotland, Estelle Quick of Tain and District Museums, and to Barbara Crawford and Simon Taylor of St Andrews University, for providing their expert comments on the text. I am also grateful to Jackie Henrie for her copy-editing expertise. Thanks are also due to Monica Kendall and Naomi Roth of Batsford, and I am especially grateful to David Breeze, the series editor, for all of his positive and generous encouragement along the way.

But my special thanks must go to my wife Sarah, and my children Holly and Christie, who had to put up with an absentee father throughout this journey.

I am grateful to the following bodies and individuals who hold copyright, and have kindly granted permission for their illustrations to be reproduced:

3, Cambridge University Library; **5 and 73**, Stewart Cruden; **13**, Tom E. Gray; **16 and colour plate 10**, Society of Antiquaries of Scotland; **17**, Edinburgh University Library; **18 and 25**, D. Pollock and the Whithorn Trust; **29b**, Whithorn Trust; **22, 45, 64, 66, 68, colour plates 1 and 11**, Trustees of the National Museums of Scotland; **29a, c, and d, 39a, b and e, 91a, b and d**, Trustees of the National Museums of Scotland and Historic Scotland; **colour plate 6**, Trustees of the National Library of Scotland; **33** Ian G. Scott, Historic Scotland and the Royal Commission on the Ancient and Historical Monuments of Scotland (RCAHMS); **34**, Faber and Faber Ltd; **36 and 79**, author; **37, 38, 43, 50, 55, 57–9, 61–3, 82, colour plates 3 and 9**, Crown copyright: RCAHMS; **40, 49, 90b and colour plate 7**, Fife Council; **41**, Lesley Donald; **51**, Dunfermline Heritage Trust; **53**, The Iona Community; **54**, Iona Cathedral Trust; **67**, National Museum of Ireland; **69**, Ulster Museum; **70**, Niall M. Robertson; **72 and 75**, Orkney Museums; **78**, Orkney Libraries; **80**, Tain and District Museums; **83** David Cemery; **85** Mick Sharp and Jean Williamson; **86** Mick Sharp; **88**, Innes Review; **92**, Whitekirk to Haddington Pigrimage Committee; **colour plate 12**, Österreiches Staatsbiblioteck, Vienna. The pilgrims' badges and *ampullae* from Perth in illustrations **39** and **89–91** are reproduced courtesy of Historic Scotland and Perth Museum and Art Gallery, Perth & Kinross Council. Illustrations **4, 9, 15, 47, and 71** are from R. W. Billings *The Baronial and Ecclesiastical Antiquities of Scotland*, 1845–52. All other illustrations are copyright Historic Scotland.

Foreword

History is often a mission of recovery. What to past generations would have seemed familiar or even commonplace can often now be forgotten or mistaken. The twentieth century's rediscovery of the pilgrimage is remarkable, but little is known by most modern pilgrims of the devotion, motivation or sheer stamina of generations of their forebears. This is particularly so in Scotland, although it for centuries glorified in its description as 'special daughter' of Rome. There is a simple reason for this: remarkably, no full-length study of Scotland's pilgrimage existed before this book.

Peter Yeoman takes the reader on a voyage across the face of Scotland, from Whithorn in the far south-west to Tain in the north – two of what were called the 'head pilgrimages of Scotland' – and beyond, to the great shrine dedicated to Earl Magnus at Kirkwall, in Orkney. In the process, almost thirty pilgrimage centres are described. The reader is also taken on a journey through more than a thousand years of Scotland's history, from the first pilgrim shrines, such as St Ninian at Whithorn or St Miren at Paisley, built probably in the fifth or sixth centuries, to others, such as the Loretto shrine at Musselburgh, founded on the eve of the Reformation. The *experience* of the medieval pilgrim is recreated by giving new meaning to what for many today must be a familiar sight – the view of Glasgow Cathedral from its great west door, where the penitent would have entered and caught their first glimpse of the altar and shrine of St Kentigern.

Remarkably, more is still being discovered – whether the fragments of a shrine, with the Cistercian rose motif and encircled cross recently found at the popular shrine dedicated to Our Lady at Whitekirk in East Lothian, or the scallop shell from the great pilgrim centre of Compostela in northern Spain found in the mouth of a man buried before the high altar on the Isle of May in the Forth. Here the author, drawing on his experience as a practising archaeologist combines new information on finds with a knowledge of ecclesiastical buildings and how they actually worked. The result is a very satisfying one. He has recreated a world which has largely been lost – the spiritual life of medieval Scots.

Professor Michael Lynch,
Dept of Scottish History
University of Edinburgh

1
To be a pilgrim

Pilgrimage in Scotland probably originated in the times when early Christianity needed to be bolstered by the power of the saints. The Church was conscious of the need to align the attributes of the spirits and deities of pre-Christian times, with the attributes of the saints, helping to make Christianity more palatable for newly converted peoples. Thus the saints played a vital role, as the historian Peter Brown has stated, in 'negotiating the honourable surrender of the old gods'. The development of the early cults of saints was further encouraged by the papacy in the eighth–ninth centuries, when they approved the dispersal of relics, especially from Rome, their purpose being to help strengthen the faith of newly converted peoples. Scotland had its fair share of the patronage of saints, ranging from an apostle of Christ, to national, indigenous saints such as Ninian, Columba and Kentigern, to a multiplicity of lesser holy men and martyrs. Saints, even the Apostles, were familiar friends and heavenly physicians, not aloof and distant entities. Their presence was palpable, ever-present, and so it is not surprising to find them, in the form of their relics, being used as powerful witnesses to legal transactions and vows . They were partners in reciprocal relationships. This was sympathetic magic which could be easily understood by all.

The approach adopted in this book is not to question the reality of the saints or the legitimacy of their relics. That they were held to be real by the medieval population is sufficient.

This is not a rewriting of the lives of the saints, or an examination of their miracles. Instead, this book is concerned with the archaeology of pilgrimage, and how an appreciation of this can help us to better understand the all-pervading nature of religion and belief in everyday life in medieval Scotland. To understand this, is to understand medieval life, especially as expressed through the archaeological and architectural fragments which we have inherited. These represent only the props, but it is religion which can provide at least some of the script.

The constant, supernatural intervention of God and the saints was believed to be all that separated mankind from tumbling into the hellish abyss. The saints provided a means of intercession, that is, they carried to God the prayers and wishes of the faithful, who were seeking stability and reassurance. Thus ordinary people could attempt to control the unpredictable world of the present and the future. The proper channel for such prayers was through the relics of the saints, both their primary corporeal remains, and their secondary artefacts of clothing, books, and so on. Pilgrimage provides us with a helpful image of the central theme of medieval life, common to all across national boundaries – the need to attain salvation to avoid the fiery pit, which was a very real and literal concept. Medieval life therefore can be seen as a journey to save the immortal soul, with pilgrimage as a specific means of making a real and difficult journey to

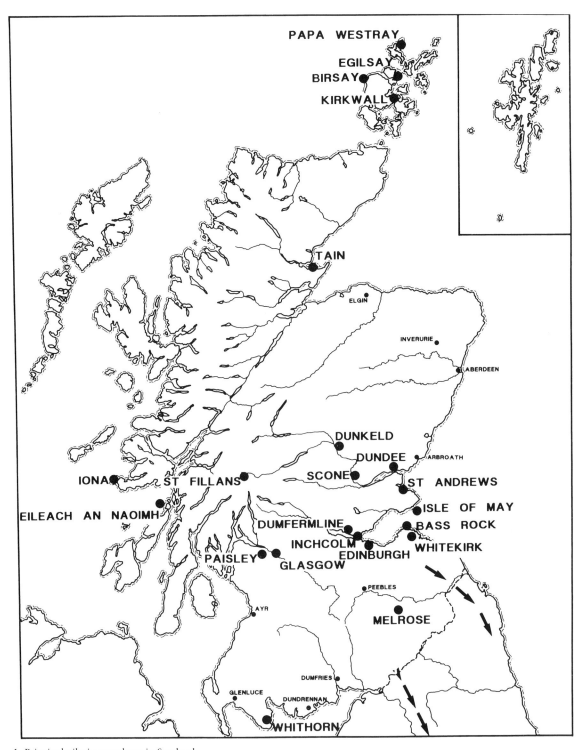

1 Principal pilgrimage places in Scotland.

achieve this. Their motivation is easy to understand – their actions, so long as they were undertaken in a spirit of devotion, would bring tangible results. They departed as penitents to expiate a crime, to seek a cure, or to fulfil a vow made in extremis. Most important of all, within a guilt-ridden society, was the need to be granted remission of sin. The harder the journey, and the greater the offering made at the end of the journey, the greater the benefit to the soul. This tangible benefit often took the form of an *indulgence*, that is a specified reduction of 'the time a soul spent being purged and cleansed in purgatory for sins committed in this life,' as defined by the historian Daphne Brooke.

Our understanding of the fabric of the medieval world can be informed by the practicalities of pilgrimage. The pilgrim had to obtain written permission from the parish priest; safe conducts were needed for foreign travel; wealth was entrusted to the king or to a great church; wives were empowered to run their affairs. We can learn about travel infrastructure, about accommodation, about victualling, and almsgiving. We can postulate how international contact helped the development and movement of ideas and innovation, as well as encouraging trade and diplomacy. The first concept of a common Europe was expressed through pilgrimage, in which many nations shared the same aspirations. There was also a universality of pilgrims' costume, which included a heavy cloak, a wide-brimmed hat often decorated with badges acquired at shrines along the way, a wooden staff with a water carrier attached, along with a small satchel called a scrip (**2**).

The cult of saints helps us understand the design and function of medieval churches and cathedrals, not just their use in the sometimes exclusive worship of monks or clergy, but also their role in popular religion. Great reliquary churches, as Professor Archie Duncan of the University of Glasgow has suggested, were built as a housing for the relics of the saint, thus making them available to the faithful. All of the chief centres of ecclesiastical organization in Scotland

2 A medieval pilgrim, with wide-brimmed hat, staff and scrip.

were given credibility by possessing the relics of the saints. Activities were not just centred on the mysteries of the sacraments, but also on the power which leaked from shrines, which was the power of the Holy Spirit on earth contained in relics. The reliquary churches provided an appropriate ritual arena allowing this supernatural power to be accessible to everyone.

3 Entombment of Edward the Confessor, with pilgrims
crawling into the tomb base.

A difficult balance had to be struck by the
church officials to reconcile the twin needs of
the security and accessibility of important relics.
This required the ritual elevation of the buried
remains of saints to be placed within a suitable
container at ground level. Access, however, had
to be limited and controlled, which resulted in
much of the activity being centred on special
feast days (3). The psychological effect was
often heightened by displaying relics in intimate
surroundings, where the movement of devotees
could be controlled by stone or timber screens.
Decoration and lighting were used to good
effect within the feretory, that is the bay or
chapel within a church assigned for the keeping
of important relics or a shrine, usually to the

east of the high altar. Crypts were built at
Whithorn, Glasgow and Iona, creating
atmospheric, enclosed spaces where the aura of
the tomb would be contained and concentrated.
Thus the stage was set for miracles of healing,
the character of which stemmed from the
biblical life of Jesus.

Saints and their relics were used to achieve
political ends, often with Church and State in
conspiracy. Corporate identification with saints
was used to reinforce concepts of national
identity during troubled times. This happened
specifically during the creation of the emergent
kingdom of Alba in the ninth century, and again
during and after the Wars of Independence
when the cult of St Andrew was manipulated to
good effect. In the fifteenth and sixteenth
centuries, adoption by the Crown of the cults of
St Duthac in Ross and St Ninian in Galloway,

aided the absorption of these previously independent regions into the nation. Another feature of this time was the wider promotion of native cults to help provide a strong, separate identity for the Scottish church. Bishop Elphinstone of Aberdeen was instrumental in achieving this by the publication of liturgical books, notably his *Aberdeen Martyrology and Breviary*, when he employed researchers to travel around compiling information on the shrines, and recording the lives of the saints. As a result of this, there was a revival of interest in the cults and an accompanying revival of pilgrimage towards the end of the medieval period. But the chief purpose of identifying and promoting the cults was to enable Scotland to present itself to the Papacy as a modern, sovereign state.

Sadly, these marvellous shrines, described wherever possible in this book, were almost completely destroyed within a short period of time around 1559 and 1560, due to the reforming zeal of the Protestant cause. The abuse of indulgences, whereby paradise could be purchased from priests and pardoners, and what came to be seen as the worthlessness of pilgrimage, had been contributory factors in the birth of the Reformation.

2
Saints and shrines in Strathclyde

St Kentigern and Glasgow Cathedral

St Kentigern's Cathedral in Glasgow is the most beautiful and complete of the larger medieval churches to survive in central Scotland today (4). It provides a classic example of how the practice of the cult of a saint could be the driving force behind the development and physical appearance of a great church. It is possible that the tomb is in its original seventh-century location, having had successive churches built around it, enabling the creation of a unique semi-subterranean cult focus.

The first historical record of Kentigern is the note of his death in a Welsh chronicle, the *Annales Cambriae*, around the year 612. There is then a significant gap of around 550 years until two Lives (*Vitae*) were written, one in 1160 and another in 1180. The name Kentigern is British in origin, meaning 'hound-lord'. His nickname, Mungo, was a diminutive which probably meant 'dear beloved'. He was reputed to be the son of St Thenew, also known as Enoch, who was daughter of the King of Lothian. His legend states that he had been brought up in St Serf's monastery at Culross in west Fife during the sixth century, although there is a small chronological difficulty here, in that the historical Serf is widely believed to have arrived in Scotland at least 100 years after this time. According to the legend, Kentigern left Culross with the intention of establishing his own community, and travelled to somewhere near Stirling by means of a miraculous parting

of the waters of the Forth. Here he was led to Glasgow, then named *Cathures*, by the cart carrying the body of Fergus, a holy man (not the saint whose head shrine was in Scone). Fergus' wish had been to be buried in a cemetery reputed to have been consecrated by St Ninian, which then became known as *cathir Fergus*, 'the enclosure of Fergus'. This may already have been the site of a timber chapel, and the focus for the local Christians who persuaded Kentigern to become their bishop. The traditional place of Fergus' burial was still recognized in the twelfth century, and may have eventually been enclosed within the Blacader Aisle at Glasgow Cathedral, as suggested in an inscription in the vaulting of about 1500 at the entrance to the aisle, which can still be seen today.

It is believed that Kentigern founded a new church here by the Molendinar burn, in *Glascu* the 'green hollow', a name which accurately describes the original setting, located a few kilometres from the royal residence of the British Kings of Strathclyde at Partick. The secular settlement, 1 km (0.6 miles) to the south on the north side of the Clyde, had grown up around a major route between north-west Scotland and the south. The road between the riverside market core and Kentigern's church became the High Street axis of the medieval burgh. Not only was Kentigern active in evangelizing the Strathclyde British, but the concentrations of dedications in Annandale,

4 The two-storey east end of Glasgow Cathedral, with part of the Blacader Aisle to the left.

Dumfriesshire and Cumbria might also indicate his physical presence in these areas. He is believed to have died around 612 and was buried in the church of his monastery in Glasgow, which soon became a place of pilgrimage.

The miracle of Somerled's defeat

An event which considerably boosted the status of St Kentigern took place in 1164, when the dread news of the approach up the Clyde of a fleet led by Somerled, the great Lord of the Isles, reached Bishop Herbert while he was in residence in a palace outside Glasgow. The attacking force landed at Renfrew, while the initial prayers by the Bishop and his largely Anglo-Norman clergy went unanswered. But Herbert was prevailed upon to return to his cathedral and pray again, no doubt at Kentigern's tomb, at which time the saint stirred, miraculously aiding the people of Glasgow, forming part of the force commanded by Walter Fitz Alan, in defeating the men of the Isles. Somerled's severed head was delivered to the Bishop, who immediately attributed the victory to Kentigern, while also proclaiming his enthusiasm for the power of the Scottish saints in general, proclaiming that '...the Scottish saints are truly to be praised!'.

The development of the cult

In the tenth and eleventh centuries the pre-eminent religious centre in this area was across the Clyde at Govan, in a royal church which contained the shrine of St Constantine (see page 00). But it was Glasgow which emerged as the seat of the diocese, as created by Earl David (later to be David I) at some time between 1113 and 1124. Govan was simply not politically acceptable to David, as this was the cult centre of the old royal dynasty. Having ruled Strathclyde and Cumbria before becoming King he was well acquainted with Kentigern's cult. It was David who was largely responsible for the revival of the cult, by greatly increasing the endowments of the cathedral, and this patronage continued during the episcopacy of Bishop John, who had been the King's own chaplain. The site of Kentigern's tomb probably remained constant, and it was around this which subsequent building phases were designed.

In about 1180 Bishop Jocelin commissioned a new *Life of Kentigern* from a monk of Furness, whose name was also Jocelin. This act of the Bishop emphasizes the foresight and faith required by medieval church builders: this *Life* was commissioned in advance of the dedication of his new church, which took place in 1197 although it was probably never finished. A newly written *Life*, complete with miracle stories, was essential to magnify and to broadcast the importance of the saint, and to thereby attract adherents along with their rich offerings to fund the building works. Bishop Jocelin had risen from being a monk, and latterly Abbot of Melrose where he had promoted the cult of St Waltheof. This coincided with the martyrdom of Thomas Becket at Canterbury in 1170. It is impossible to underestimate how important this martyr, the first for hundreds of years, was for the Church. Martyrs were especially blessed and went straight to heaven; therefore Becket's saintly powers of intercession and miracles were held to be immensely strong. Jocelin's experience in the promotion of the cult of Waltheof was an ideal qualification when he became Bishop of Glasgow in 1174, when he immediately set about doing the same for Kentigern. Waltheof was of royal kin, and so Jocelin's support would not have gone unnoticed by the King.

Bishop Jocelin needed to create a powerfully attractive cult around St Kentigern, not least to escape the threat to succumb to the supremacy of the Archbishop of York, as the Whithorn diocese had done. The presence of the relics of an important saint reinforced the case for Glasgow, which was successful in lobbying the Pope to designate Glasgow as a special daughter of Rome – in other words, under the direct authority of the Pope, rather than that of an

English prelate. This status was extended to the whole of the Scottish church in 1176, confirming ecclesiastical independence from England. There was a major problem however, caused by the pronouncement of Pope Alexander III in 1170, that no saint could be venerated unless properly canonized by the papacy. Relics alone were not enough, and hence Jocelin of Furness was commissioned to write the new *Life*, detailing the saint's asceticism and miracles, essentially as a promotional document to support the case for canonization. In the *Life*, the writer honestly stated that he had looked in vain for any posthumous miracles of Kentigern, which was certainly not what the Bishop required, and so no doubt Jocelin of Furness was persuaded to add a chapter detailing the requisite, showy Irish-style miracles. The Bishop knew that he needed to translate the bones of his saint into a wonderful shrine, involving the arrangements he had witnessed when he had been present in Clairvaux at the translation of St Bernard in 1175. But even with a carefully orchestrated campaign, no canonization was forthcoming.

However, all this does not seem to have dissuaded Bishop Jocelin from his steady path of promoting the cult, fired no doubt by the great devotion of the age, the veneration of the martyr-saint, Thomas Becket, at Canterbury. Jocelin can be seen to have purposefully set about promoting Kentigern in parallel with St Thomas, possibly with the encouragement of King William the Lion, who founded Arbroath Abbey in 1178 in honour of the martyr. The Bishop is likely to have visited the tomb of St Thomas at Canterbury, establishing close links between the two cathedrals. Recent archaeological excavations have shown that Jocelin's rebuilding featured not only the enlargement of the nave, but also perhaps the raising of this to enable the creation of the first two-storey arrangement at the east end with the tomb chapel (incorporating the original east end of the earlier church) transformed into a complete under-church, allowing for a raised

choir above (5). The design was inextricably linked to the drama of veneration, and the practicalities of controlling the visibility of relics and the movement of pilgrims within sacred space. It is sometimes stated that the two-storey east end arrangement was largely driven by the practical need to overcome the difficulties of a sloping site. But this was a minor consideration, and in fact 'the siting of the crypt was determined by the desire to create the most splendid pilgrimage site in the country'.

The obvious parallel can be drawn between Kentigern's tomb and the original tomb of St Thomas, on the floor of the crypt beneath the choir at Canterbury. Like Glasgow, the crypts at Canterbury, Winchester, Gloucester and Worcester took the form of complete under-churches, the use of crypts harking back to the Gregorian remodelling of Old St Peter's in Rome c 600. And the St Thomas connection did not end there; the cathedral's Treasury inventory of 1432 lists amongst its relics 'the shirts of St Kentigern and St Thomas, and the combs of St Kentigern and St Thomas'. Presumably this means that at some time a Glasgow bishop, possibly Jocelin, was successful in obtaining relics of the martyr to help boost the scale of pilgrimage and devotion. There was a separate chapel and altar dedicated to St Thomas in Glasgow Cathedral, where his relics would have been displayed, particularly on his feast days. A document of 1320 records the gift of a fine set of vestments to be used during these services.

It is likely that Bishop Jocelin opened the tomb to remove the relics of Kentigern, even without the papal authority of canonization, to enable a new shrine to be installed behind the high altar of his raised choir, at the time of the dedication of his magnificent remodelling in 1197. The cathedral was magnified once more by Bishop William Bondington (1233–58), who was responsible for commissioning the next large-scale rebuilding, including an enlarged east end to accommodate the high altar and a new chapel for St Kentigern's shrine. The empty

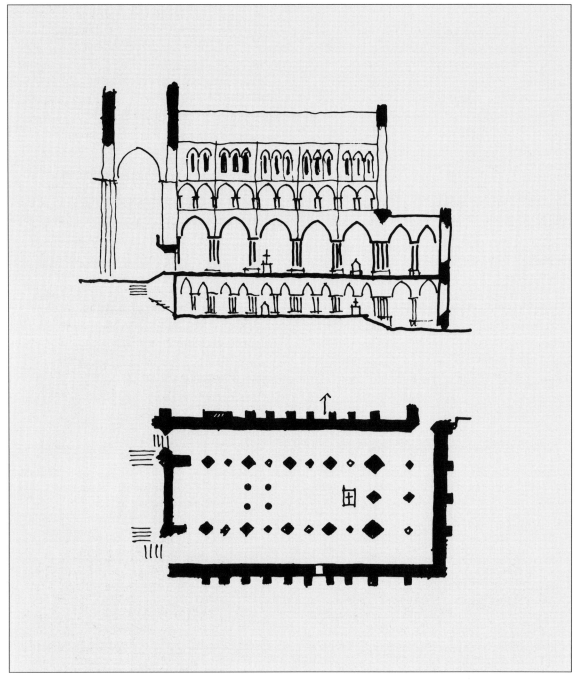

5 Sketch section of the east end of Glasgow Cathedral, and plan of the laigh or under-church, showing the arrangement of principal altars and shrines: high altar with the shrine of St Kentigern behind in the presbytery, corresponding with the saint's tomb backed by the altar of Our Lady in the lower church.

tomb below remained a focus of the cult, again echoing the situation in Canterbury where St Thomas' empty tomb continued to play an important role within the cult long after the translation of the body in 1220. This conscious imitation was reinforced by Bishop Bondington, whose thirteenth-century rebuilding provided the vaulting strongly reminiscent of the arched canopy above Thomas' tomb illustrated in a contemporary window at Canterbury. Further examples of this arrangement can be seen at Lindisfarne Priory where the empty tomb of Cuthbert was venerated, as was the case with Columba's tomb at Iona.

But what did Kentigern's tomb and shrine look like? The obverse of the Chapter Seal of the later thirteenth century, in use at the time of Bishop Robert Wishart, shows a model church with a central spire resting on a triple-arched structure, rising behind an altar. The reverse depicts another raised platform on top of which is the bust of a stern-faced, bearded and mitred bishop, holding his right hand up in benediction, and flanked by a pair of low spires (6). Beneath the platform, framed by triple arches, are three kneeling or crawling figures wearing unusual hats, praying to the bust. Part of the inscription can be translated as 'Dear Kentigern, bless your servants'. Remarkable as it

6 Thirteenth century Chapter Seal of Glasgow Cathedral. Reverse (left) possibly showing pilgrims at the tomb, obverse (right) possibly depicting the shrine.

may seem, it is likely that we are being shown a contemporary representation of both the shrine and the tomb below. The front of the seal may well show the beautifully made wooden box or *chasse*, in the form of a church as was often the case, displayed on a raised platform behind the high altar. It is even possible that the reverse shows an image of a head shrine reliquary of Kentigern, atop the empty tomb, being venerated by pilgrims. A fairly portable relic, such as this head shrine, was ideal for the purposes of procession, both within and outside the church, especially on the saint's feast days. Or could this image represent part of a tomb-effigy of the saint which lay on the empty tomb? That the crypt below and the shrine above were both of considerable importance, and formed a persistent twin focus for veneration, is reinforced by the fact that when Edward I visited in 1301 he made offerings at the tomb and shrine of the saint, as detailed in his wardrobe accounts.

In 1420, Bishop William Lauder successfully petitioned the Pope to replace the old shrine with a new chest of gold or silver, 'that they (the relics) be more devoutly honoured' (7). This act

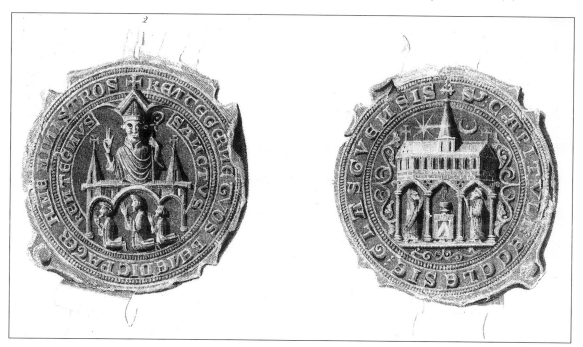

7 Reconstruction drawing of the shrine of St Kentigern in the upper church at Glasgow Cathedral, with devotees under the watchful eyes of cathedral officials (drawn by David Simon).

can be related to the need to attract increased revenues to help fund rebuilding following serious damage caused to the cathedral by a lightning strike in 1400.

The experience of the pilgrim at Glasgow

What is so exciting about this place is that the modern visitor can easily replicate the experience of the medieval pilgrim, thanks to the almost complete preservation of the architecture of the later medieval church (8). The bishops and their masons, through the various building campaigns, had crafted a design which clearly mapped the path to be taken by the pilgrims from the moment they entered from the west, while at the same time heightening the anticipation and the drama of

the experience at appropriate points along the way. The sophisticated design enabled this without causing disruption to the canons carrying out their daily round of services. At busy times, the natural flow of traffic determined by the careful spatial planning could be marshalled and regulated by cathedral officials. One of the most senior of these was the Treasurer who was charged with keeping the necessary equipment, furnishings and treasures in good repair. At the upper level, the focus of light, incense, statuary, and precious metals around the elevated position of the shrine would have drawn the pilgrims around the aisles to the north and south of the choir, to either gain access to, or to simply view, the shrine in the feretory bay beyond the high altar, also dedicated to St Kentigern. The reredos panels behind the high altar would not have been so high as to obscure the shrine when viewed by worshippers in the west part of the church. The decoration around the shrine was varied, and probably included tapestries such as the arras illustrating the life of the saint listed in the 1432 cathedral inventory. A one-way system may have operated to bring the pilgrim out of the south aisle to then follow the processional route down the gloomy steps and into the south aisle of the crypt (**9**).

Here the upper arrangement of especially sacred features – high altar and shrine – was precisely mirrored by the location of the tomb and the altar to the Virgin. But the real surprise for the pilgrim was the light; natural light from the windows, along with candle light, was

8 Reconstruction drawing of pilgrims at the tomb of St Kentigern on a feast day, when the gates around the tomb were opened allowing direct contact with the sepulchre. The metal gates are adorned with ex-votos and crutches left there by the healed and by those seeking cures (drawn by David Simon).

carefully managed to emphasize the tomb under its vaulted canopy with enriched ribs and bosses. This would originally have been further highlighted by brightly painted decoration on the stonework (**10**). The vaulting is a triumph of the medieval mason's craft, because not only did it serve to mark and glorify the tomb, but it was also essential in helping support the great bulk of the upper church. Having come down the steps, the astonished pilgrims could perform their devotions at the tomb, and then move on to the highly prestigious Lady Chapel dedicated to the Virgin, before descending more steps to the east to arrive at the ambulatory with four chapels, one each dedicated to St Andrew, St Nicholas, St Peter St Paul, and St John the Evangelist. They could also make their devotions here before starting the ascent and retracing their steps around the north aisle of the crypt, passing once again by the Lady Chapel and the tomb. There

9 The south aisle passage at Glasgow Cathedral which
formed part of the ambulatory enabling pilgrims to move
between the shrine in the east end of the upper church,
and the stairs down to the tomb in the lower church, and
the Blacader Aisle (*cathir Fergus*).

was direct access in and out of the crypt by way
of doors, centrally placed to north and south.
Although the space was cleverly managed, there
would undoubtedly be congestion when large
crowds attended on feast days, when the crush of
bodies in the claustrophobic space could easily
have prompted panic, especially among the old
and the sick, and others in a frenzied state
having experienced miraculous cures.

Like so many saints, Kentigern had more
than one annual festival, the main one being
celebrated on 13 January. In addition, towards
the end of the twelfth century, Bishop Jocelin
had established a week-long fair to mark the
Feast of the Dedication, and this holiday in July

is observed by Glaswegians to this day. We
know little of the quantified benefits to the souls
of the pilgrims when visiting at certain times,
apart from the indulgence of 40 days off
purgatory for those visiting the cathedral during
the Feast of the Dedication, granted by the Pope
to Bishop Lauder in 1420. We also have little
idea of the extent to which relics were
processed, inside and outside the cathedral,
although it does seem likely that the great feasts
would warrant such outings. It is known that
Bishop Herbert introduced the Sarum Ritual
from Salisbury to Glasgow in 1147; this defined
the full liturgical practice of a great church and
involved a considerable degree of processing.

The experience of the pilgrim was not
restricted solely to the cathedral, however, as

10 The site of St Kentigern's tomb as it is today, with
vaulting over, and the chapels at the lower level to
the east.

those coming from further afield required accommodation, and the poor may have depended on alms to support themselves during their visit. The cathedral, although lacking a cloister, nevertheless had a magnificent setting within the precinct, which enclosed the church, restricted on the east side by the steep slope down to the Molendinar Burn. On the other three sides were the Bishop's Castle, numerous manses to house the canons (latterly 32 in number), as well as other related buildings including hospitals and almshouses (**11**). A hospital was founded in 1503 to accommodate 'poor travellers', often a synonym for pilgrims, at the Stablegreen Port, just to the north of the Bishop's Castle. Here the canons were careful not to mix up their two large

pots, one for cooking with, and the other for washing the feet of the poor! Near the hospital was the bishop's almshouse, overseen by a priest whose residence, now called Provand's Lordship, survives to this day.

The wealthier pilgrims would have found food and lodgings in inns within the burgh to the south, and elsewhere outwith the precinct. Whilst here, they could visit a lesser shrine, that of the saint's mother, Thenew, whose cult also developed in Glasgow based around her tomb at the church dedicated to her (now given her alternative name, St Enoch's) at the west end of the Trongate. Offerings here were sufficient to pay for her shrine to be renewed at some time during the fifteenth century. St Thenew's Well stood near to the chapel, and when this was cleaned out in the nineteenth century, it was found to contain several ex-votos. Ex-votos are representations of limbs or organs, or sometimes the whole body, carved in wood or wax, which were often encountered adorning shrines. They represented the part which needed to be healed, or else the part which had been healed. Ex-votos can still be seen at continental shrines to this day.

11 The precinct of Glasgow Cathedral in the late medieval period, with the High Street leading to the Mercat Cross in the top left of the picture. The buttressed chapel of St Nicholas' hospital is shown to the left of the Bishop's Castle. Other pilgrims' hospitals and almshouses were also located in the same row. The Cathedral is flanked by the manses and chambers of the principal officials and canons.

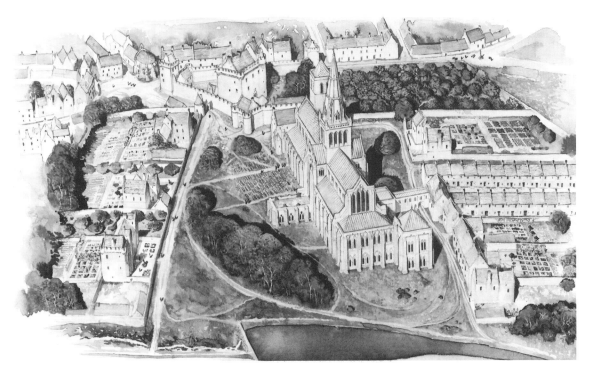

The list of relics

The inventory of 1432 contains a record of other relics additional to those of St Kentigern and St Thomas already mentioned. Most of the relics are likely to have already been in the cathedral treasury for centuries before they were listed. Included are relics which would only be found in the highest ranking continental churches: two silver crosses containing pieces of the True Cross; reliquaries containing hair and milk of the Blessed Virgin (the latter often brought back from the Holy Land by Crusaders); part of the manger of the Lord; and a phial with oil distilled from the tomb of St Kentigern. The inventory also lists offerings to the saint which had not yet been utilized including 'precious stones of ruby colour for the shrine of St Kentigern'. Another relic of the saint, which was not listed, was his hand-bell which had to be rung through the streets of Glasgow the night before certain festivals.

Some of these relics, along with some of the other cathedral treasures, were in the possession of Archbishop James Beaton when he fled to France in 1560. Their subsequent fate is uncertain.

Investigations in the lower church

The area of the tomb consists of a low raised stone platform, upon which the tomb superstructure originally stood. This was excavated in 1898, but without any significant results – the platform rested on natural subsoil, and any bones that were still here in the sixteenth century would have been destroyed by the zealous adherents of the Reformation. It is believed that the tomb had been close to the extreme east end of the earliest churches, and these excavations purported to have revealed the curving east end apse wall which enclosed the tomb and marked the east end into the twelfth century.

A fascinating discovery was made in the bay furthest to the west. Excavations in 1978 uncovered a circular stone-lined cistern or basin, 0.5 m (1.6 ft) in diameter, axially located 13 m (40 ft) from the tomb with a lead pipe supply. This may have been related in some way to the other unusual water feature of the crypt – the well in the furthest south-east corner sited in one of the lower eastern chapels. The well is likely to have been fed by an ancient spring long associated with the saint, and it is interesting to note that a similar arrangement existed at St Andrews. It would have been common to have a water source with healing properties next to a shrine, and both sources in the crypt could have been used by the pilgrims to fill their *ampullae* with holy water. The cistern, however, may have had a more complicated function in relation to the ceremonial of the tomb, or it could have been a *piscina* drain.

Another pilgrimage-related structure which can still be seen, now located close to the well, is a length of finely carved thirteenth-century stone arcading, which for some time was believed to form part of either the base of the shrine or of the tomb (**12**). If this interpretation is wrong, then these fragments are still helpful in exemplifying stone and timber arcading, now gone, which would have been necessary to contain the pilgrims, while simultaneously allowing them glimpses of the sacred structures.

The importance of the cult

This seems to have been a cult which was largely restricted to the west of Scotland, although the dearth of surviving documents makes it difficult to know the numbers of pilgrims, or how far they travelled to venerate St Kentigern and to pray for his intercession. It can be suggested that the high points of his cult correspond directly with the major building campaigns of the twelfth and fifteenth centuries, and at the time of the successful supplication to Rome in 1492 to achieve archdiocese status, times when the bishops most needed to be associated with a seemingly important saint, and when they were in greatest need of the revenues which this could provide. The non-completion of the south (Blacader) aisle extension, intended since the thirteenth century as an even more magnificent two-storey setting for the shrine, coupled with a recorded decline in lay benefactions, might indicate that the revival of the cult in the fifteenth

12 Possible remains of the thirteenth-century base of
    St Kentigern's shrine.

century was unsuccessful. Edward I of England was the only King known to have made offerings at the shrine, and possibly because of this no Scottish royal gifts are recorded, other than the favours of David I, who presumably had acted at least partly out of devotion to Kentigern. James IV, however, did also favour the cathedral, having become a canon at an early age.

St Constantine of Govan

The combined political and cultural power of Church and State, in the context of an early cult site, are well illustrated by the remarkable collection of the products of the 'Govan school' of stone-carving, dating from the ninth to the twelfth century. The most important of these is the so-called sarcophagus of St Constantine (**13**).

We know little of the fortunes of Kentigern's church in Glasgow before the twelfth-century revival, except to say that it was overshadowed by the cult centre at nearby Govan, on the south side of the Clyde, 5 km (3 miles) to the west. The precise identity of St Constantine is uncertain; he could be a conflation of the legends of two or three separate holy men of that name, or more

13 The Govan sarcophagus.

CONSTANTINE K. AND M. FOVNDER OF GOVAN CHVRCH A.D. 576. PRESERVED WITHIN THE

likely, he was a dynastic saint of the Scottish royal house, which included a number of Constantines at the end of the ninth century. It is even possible that the individual commemorated at Govan is the same Constantine recorded in the inscription on the Dupplin Cross. The consolidation of the Scottish take-over of the British kingdom of Strathclyde at this time would have benefited from the creation of a new cult focus, located at what had probably already been a royal church of the Strathclyde British, close to long-established royal centres at Dumbarton and Partick.

The nineteenth-century parish church stands within a large curvilinear burial ground, a plan which is characteristic of early Christian monastic enclosures, and recent excavations have indeed located a medieval church below the standing church, more centrally placed within the enclosure. These investigations have also revealed the site of a contemporary royal palace just to the east of the monastic enclosure, the two possibly being linked by a processional way. The newly discovered medieval church is likely to have replaced an older church which would have housed the early commemorative sculpted stones, including the remarkable sarcophagus which features a central stag-hunting scene with a single mounted huntsman. This may be a royal portrait, but there is no certainty that this represents St Constantine, as this is the only surviving one of three sarcophagi, found in 1762 in the furthest south-east corner of the graveyard. They must have been disposed of here after having been cleared out of the church after the Reformation. The surviving stone coffin, as presumably were the others, was designed to be viewed from all sides, and therefore must have stood above-ground, following the continental royal fashion which can be traced back to the re-use of ornate Roman sarcophagi.

It is quite possible that this was a cult reliquary for a royal burial, which provided a twin focus alongside the high altar. This cult existed on royal patronage, and probably died immediately after this patronage shifted to Kentigern in the early twelfth century. There is no evidence of pilgrimage to Govan in later medieval times.

St Conval of Inchinnan

Inchinnan, a post-industrial conurbation, 7 km (4.3 miles) upstream from Govan and close to Glasgow Airport, had been the place of arrival of a sixth-century Irish missionary named Conval, who is reputed to have been a contemporary of Kentigern and has been described as his 'first archdeacon'. The place-name Inchinnan means 'Island of the Rivers', being enclosed on three sides by the Rivers Clyde, Black Cart and Gryfe. An alternative meaning is 'St Finnian's Isle', recording the original patron who was later replaced in tradition by St Conval. The Conval legend has it that the saint pitched up here, having prayed with such fervour that the block of granite upon which he was standing carried him across the Irish Sea and up the Clyde. This stone, called St Conval's Chariot, was reputed to have miraculous healing powers for sick people and cattle; the stone can still be seen nearby (see page 92). His festival was celebrated on 28 September.

The old parish church which grew up on the site of his tomb was demolished to make way for the airport, but the new parish church still houses an important group of cross-slabs, dated to the tenth to twelfth century, which are more products of the Govan school. One of these, carved with the biblical scene of Daniel in the Lions' Den, has prominent corner bosses, reminiscent of the corner-posts of slab-built shrines, and appears to be a recumbent shrine stone, which may have covered the saint's tomb. We can never know if this formed part of the shrine revered by later medieval pilgrims, including the chronicler Hector Boece who visited around 1500. This was considered to be the mother church of Renfrewshire, and as such was afforded special treatment by David I who granted it to the Knights Templars, when all the other churches in Strathgryfe were granted to the newly created Paisley Abbey.

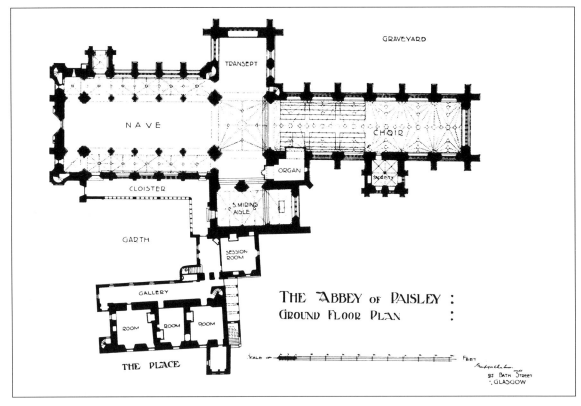

THE ABBEY OF PAISLEY :
GROUND FLOOR PLAN

St Miren of Paisley

Miren is believed to have been a noble Irishman who was instructed by St Congal at his renowned training monastery for missionaries at Bangor, Co. Down. Church dedications and local traditions have him as evangelizing around Perthshire, Angus, and Loch Lomond, as well as Renfrewshire, where his cult grew up after his death and burial at Paisley around 600. His festival was celebrated on 15 September.

As was often the case, his place of burial became the focus for a newly created monastery in the later twelfth century, the possession of Miren's relics, along with the heritage of sanctity of the site, being sufficiently attractive c 1169 to draw the colonizing convent of Cluniac monks away from their original church at Renfrew. The endowment had been created by Walter Fitz Alan after his arrival in Scotland at the behest of David I, to serve as his High Steward, thus naming and establishing the great Stewart family (**14**). Paisley was dedicated to the Virgin, as well as to two saints familiar to them from Shropshire –

14 Plan of Paisley Abbey, as rebuilt and restored early this century. St Miren's Aisle is to the south of the crossing.

St Milburga, and St James the Greater of Compostela who was already the patron saint of the Stewarts. This devotion to St James was soon to spread throughout large parts of Scotland, and was to influence the later pattern of Scots pilgrimage abroad. To these imported dedications was added the cult of St Miren; apart from having purely religious motives, it would also have been most diplomatic for incoming Anglo-Norman lords and monks to adopt the popular native saint of an area. Eventually Miren gained precedence and the other dedications were dropped.

The pilgrims' chapel and shrine of St Miren was originally located in the standard position behind the high altar, with the relics having been installed here, no doubt as part of an impressive ceremony, only a few years after the commencement of building. In the 1450s the fittings of the church were magnified by Abbot Thomas Tervas of Paisley, who went on

pilgrimage to Rome in 1453 and returned with a long list of furnishings and vestments of the highest quality, acquired at various places, including Bruges where he may have obtained 'the staitliest tabernakle in all Skotland and the maist costlie'. The Stewarts loyally maintained their support of Paisley Abbey, which was a principal place of burial for the family. Abbot George Shaw further revived interest in the saint in the later fifteenth century, and it was here in 1491, in the presence of the relics, that James IV and the others implicated in the death of his royal father received

15 St Miren's Aisle, Paisley Abbey, with the sculpted frieze of scenes from the life of the saint in the background, and the ornate tomb of Marjory Bruce (died 1316), daughter of Robert I, in the foreground.

absolution from Shaw representing the Pope. By 1499 Shaw had created a new, large pilgrims' chapel and shrine for St Miren by enlarging the thirteenth-century south transept, provided with a decorative sculpted frieze, originally brightly painted, illustrating the life of the saint, which can still be seen today (**15**). Although now a frieze,

16 Part of the fifteenth-century sculpted frieze from St
Miren's Aisle, Paisley Abbey, depicting scenes from the
life of the saint. These panels may originally have
formed part of an altar retable, that is, a decorative rear
panel behind an altar.

originally this may have formed a composite altar
retable. The miracle stories depicted in the frieze
were clearly current at the time, and are the same
as those written down a few years later in the
Aberdeen Breviary by Shaw's friend, Bishop
William Elphinstone (**16**).

It is possible that the new chapel was planned
as a two-storey arrangement, with the shrine
raised up above a crypt containing a treasury
along with the tomb of the saint. This seems
curiously similar to the plans of the same date
for the new shrine intended for Kentigern, also
in a south transept location at Glasgow, which
Shaw would have been well aware of.

Shaw's new shrine of St Miren attracted
further endowments, including one from James
Crawford and his wife Elizabeth Galbraith, of
Stirlingshire, to employ a chaplain to say daily
masses for their salvation. The abbey church
contained other shrines, including one in the
choir dedicated to Our Lady of Paisley, which
was commonly used for swearing and redeeming
financial transactions and solemn vows. By
1500, Paisley was identified as one of the four
'heid' pilgrimages, along with Melrose, Dundee
and Scone, the circuit of which was regularly
cited as a penance. Pilgrims at this time would
have been deeply impressed by another of
Shaw's achievements, the enclosure of the abbey
precinct by a high wall, about 3 km (1.9 miles)
in length and adorned with religious statues,
heraldic arms and inscriptions. The walls stood
until the late eighteenth century and were widely
regarded as one of the wonders of the land.

3
Ninian of Whithorn, and the shrines around Edinburgh and the Borders

If you visit the quiet town of Whithorn today, it is hard to believe that this was once a famed centre of international trade and worship, which grew up around the longest lasting pilgrimage place in Scotland, a focus for devotees of St Ninian for a period of around 1100 years (**17**). New historical research and 10 years of excavations around the shrine during the 1980s and 1990s, have thoroughly changed our ideas about Scotland's other patron saint. He achieved wide popularity at home and abroad, and was held dear by the Irish, the Scandinavians, the Saxons and the Scots, although the development of his cult in a nationwide context was really a phenomenon of the high middle ages. We must suspend our modern perceptions of centrality, and consider Whithorn and Galloway as an important centre, the development of which was fuelled by the cult of St Ninian (**colour plate 1**).

The traditional legend of Ninian was based on a few lines about him written down by Bede in his *Ecclesiastical History of the English Nation*, of around 731. Bede described how Ninian was taught at Rome, and spent time under St Martin of Tours who died in 397. Ninian is supposed to have returned to his native land to establish a monastery and church at Whithorn, named *Candida Casa*, possibly meaning 'shining white house', and dedicated to St Martin. A fragment of what was thought to be this church was wishfully identified in excavations earlier this century, to the east of

the later medieval cathedral. Bede also informs us that Ninian converted the southern Picts to Christianity, before his death and burial within his church in 431. Almost all of this has been called into doubt in recent research, and it is certainly the case that Bede's sources were imprecise, and that he had something to gain by talking up the cult and the place to help his friend, Pecthelm, who had just been appointed as first Northumbrian Bishop of Whithorn.

The alternative version suggests a pre-Christian origin for the *Candida Casa* place-name, and that Whithorn was already established as a centre of trade and power for the local British population, within the sphere of Roman Carlisle. This version discounts Ninian's travels to Rome and Tours, and any missionary work outwith the south-west; a church, yes, but nothing we would recognize as a monastery. What remains constant is that Ninian was a local sub-Roman Briton, who became the first Bishop at the head of the local church hierarchy; he was a holy man and miracle worker, held in great reverence by the Christian population, whose burial-place did become a focus for pilgrimage soon after his death, in the fifth or early sixth century. What was thought to be a fragment of Ninian's church is now believed to date from the eighth century.

The archaeology of the shrine
The key to understanding the development of Whithorn is to keep a clear idea of the location

17 Miniature from the *Salisbury Book of Hours*, of St
Ninian depicted holding shackles, illustrating his
attribute as a freer of captives.

of the founder's – Ninian's – tomb. The original
religious and secular centre, possibly the oldest
settlement of truly urban character in Scotland,
was on and around the hilltop where the ruined
church of the cathedral priory is sited. The only
possible location of the grave is to the east of
the crown of the hill, in the crypt of the later
medieval cathedral, and it is entirely possible
that this remained constant ever since the fifth
century, due to the extreme continuity of
reverence, coupled with the natural
conservatism of religious practice. Relics can be
and were moved regularly, but to move a grave
is a difficult proposition which would devalue
its sanctity. The development of Whithorn
from the fifth to the sixteenth century might
therefore have been predicated by this
fixed point.

The recent major campaign of excavations
was focused on the gentle southern slope of the
hillside, and not on the summit. The only clue
we have of a church on the summit, broadly
contemporary with Bishop Ninian's lifetime, is
in the form of an inscribed stone erected at
some time in the fifth century by a man named
Latinus. This was long thought to be a
gravestone, but is now best interpreted as an
inauguration stone, which stood beside the
door of a newly built church, recording the
name of the aristocratic donor. This could have
been Ninian's own church where he was
buried, or a rebuilding of this soon after his
death. The excavations revealed that the hilltop
was encircled by a ditch allowing sufficient
space for more than one church, and it is quite
possible that even by 500 the saint's relics had
been translated into a grander, reliquary
church in the western part of the summit.
Outwith the ditch was a settlement of terraced
streets of rectangular timber houses; these
streets were trod by the first pilgrims to
venerate St Ninian.

Something very curious happened at the
south-west corner of the original church
enclosure during the later sixth and into the
seventh century. Three successive outdoor
circular enclosures, labelled 'shrines' by the
excavator and clearly of ritual function, were
constructed, replacing some of the earlier
houses. These platforms became a focus for
east–west, apparently Christian, burials. The
older hilltop enclosure was enlarged to include
these features. These ritual platforms might be
associated with a period of reversion to pre-
Christian worship, or may even be from a time
when the two belief systems co-existed at
Whithorn. The platforms contained settings of
stone or timber pillars, which in the pagan
worship of late antiquity had come to symbolize
a sacred grove. An alternative explanation is
derived from the evidence of the material
culture. The people living in the early town from
the late fifth century until around 700 made
good use of high-quality pottery and glass from
the Mediterranean and from Gaul, goods which
were probably transhipped to Whithorn from
Atlantic Gaul as part of a wider trade around
the Irish Sea. Gaulish clerics may have
accompanied this trade, being attracted to a
famed shrine, and they may have been
responsible for introducing the devotion to
St Martin, possibly in the tangible form of relics
of this saint, along with exotic burial practices.

But the Gaulish influence was probably
minor compared to that of the Irish, or Iona,
style of monasticism so popular at this time, and
it is thought likely that a monastery of this kind
was created here around the saint's tomb and
shrine by the early seventh century. The
Columban monks may even have come with the
specific objective of stamping out a resurgence
of Druidical worship at a revered place of
Christian pilgrimage. It is thought that
Whithorn was established as a famous place of
religious study from the time of Ninian on, and
that Irish and British clerics came to study here.
This connection was reinforced further by the
fact that St Finnian, who was probably a Briton,

was believed to have been tutored here before travelling to the monastery at Strangford in Ulster, where he taught the young Columba around 540. We must also remember that Galloway was very much a part of the Irish Sea province, and that Ulster and Whithorn were separated only by a relatively short distance across the North Channel, where there was regular traffic by *curraghs* (ox-hide covered boats). It is therefore not surprising that the Ninianic cult was both popular with the Irish, and influenced by them, throughout many centuries.

The monastery and the shrine were transformed again during the first half of the eighth century, when Galloway fell under the control of the Anglian kingdom of Northumbria, at the time when the Northumbrian Church had rejected many of the practices introduced to them by Columban Christianity. The site was no doubt revitalized by the establishment of a Northumbrian bishopric, the first incumbent being Bede's friend, Pecthelm. Churches and other monastic buildings would still have existed on the summit, and the excavations have revealed that two timber oratories and a burial enclosure were built on the site of the older platform shrines, about 50 m (168 ft) south of the hilltop. The construction of the Northumbrian buildings was very similar to that of the fragment of the oldest surviving church at the east end of the hilltop, excavated in the 1950s, possibly indicating that the church containing Ninian's tomb was rebuilt again at this time. By around 800 the two southern oratories had been combined to form a single timber church, and the adjacent enclosure was rebuilt as a burial chapel, with windows of brightly painted glass (**18**). A central altar, which may well have contained relics, was found in the timber church. The Northumbrian church was keen to promote Roman orthodoxy, one expression of which was to dedicate churches to St Peter; indeed, another sculpted stone from Whithorn proclaims that 'this is the place of Peter the

Apostle'. Charles Thomas has gone so far as to suggest that the so-called *Petrus* stone might have stood near the timber church and 'more or less announces the acquisition of a Petrine relic', which was housed in this church, having been brought here from Rome, via Northumbria. This would have launched Whithorn to the zenith of attractiveness to pilgrims, whom the excavator believed would have been accommodated in some of the large timber halls found just to the south of the sacred buildings of the inner precinct.

Many saints were exploited to help achieve political ends, and this was especially true of the Anglian take-over of Galloway. They were pleased to accept and to embellish the cult of Ninian, and to further promote the importance of the shrine by circulating literature written by Whithorn monks during the eighth century, describing the numerous miracles. One of these works, a poem entitled *Miracula Niniae Episcopi,* provides a unique contemporary insight into the appearance of the place, describing a (presumably empty) rock-cut grave, as well as Ninian's stone reliquary sarcophagus which rested beside the altar of his main church.

The southern focus of churches was abandoned at some time during the tenth century, leaving probably just two on the hilltop. The religious settlement continued to develop with power shifting between Anglo-Saxon, Scandinavian and Irish Gaelic peoples, all sharing the common veneration of the saint, and providing the means to continue the development of the holy place. It is believed that a large cruciform cathedral church was built in the middle of the twelfth century by Fergus of Galloway on the site of the principal older church. At this time the sepulchral church housing Ninian's tomb remained as a separate building at the east end of the hilltop, although this was also absorbed into the cathedral when the east end was extended around 1200 to accommodate the liturgical needs of the Premonstratensian canons recently introduced to the cathedral priory. The difference in levels

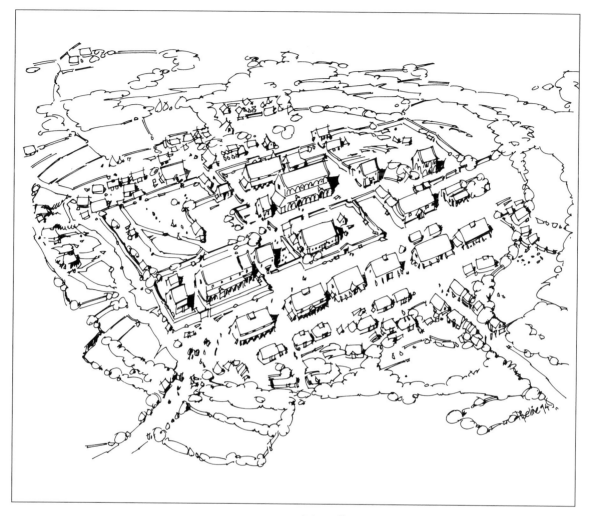

18 Reconstruction of the Northumbrian minster at Whithorn in about 800. A large church is shown on the summit of the hill to the east of which is a small separate building which may have enclosed the tomb of St Ninian; part of this building survives to the east of the later medieval cathedral. The large church in the south-west part of the enclosure was formed by conjoining two oratories.

between the two buildings meant that they were able to incorporate the west half of the sepulchral church as a crypt. The medieval builders probably believed that this older church was Ninian's *Candida Casa*, imbued with 800 years of sanctity absorbed from the saint's tomb, and now absorbed into the fabric in their new church (**19**).

Travelling to Whithorn

St Ninian attracted pilgrims from the lands around the Irish Sea and from the Continent. Contemporary accounts from the fifteenth century describe how busy the roads of Galloway were with Scots pilgrims heading south towards the Whithorn peninsula. There were various assembly points along the way where pilgrims could meet and band together. The upkeep of roads and bridges was viewed as an act of piety, a good example being the supplication made to the Pope in 1441 by Margaret, Countess of Douglas, for her to be granted an indulgence in return for offerings in support of the rebuilding of a bridge over the River Bladnoch 'where pilgrims to St Ninian assemble'. Another such *statio* was at the

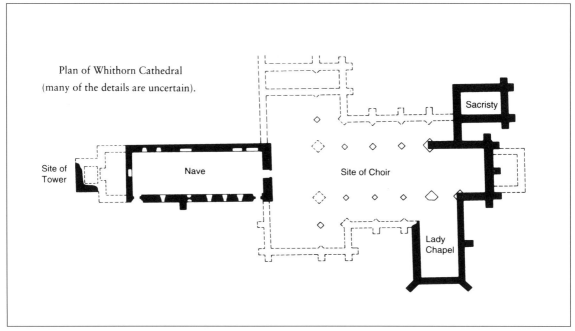

Plan of Whithorn Cathedral
(many of the details are uncertain).

Sacristy

Site of
Tower

Nave

Site of Choir

Lady
Chapel

19 Plan of the Premonstratensian cathedral priory of
Whithorn in the early sixteenth century, following the
addition of the large southern chapel.

Laggangairn standing stones, a prehistoric ritual
site and no doubt then a famous landmark, in
bleak moorland 15 km (9.3 miles) north of
Glenluce Abbey. The stones were incised with
crosses dated to the seventh to ninth century. For
a pilgrimage to be acceptable in the eyes of God
it had to involve extremes of distance, along with
the associated hardships of travel. This is well
illustrated by the encounter in July 1504 between
James IV and a group of 'puir folkis of Tayn
passand to Whithern', when James was returning
by way of Glasgow from his own pilgrimage to
St Ninian. The journey was essential; it was not
sufficient to live beside the relics of an important
saint to qualify as a pilgrim.

Many of the Scots pilgrims would have
received hospitality and alms from the
numerous religious houses in Dumfries and
Galloway, with many spending their last night
at Glenluce before reaching their goal the next
day (**81**). The monks at Dundrennan were also
involved in providing hospitality, some of which
may have been subsidized by the sale of

pilgrims' badges (*signacula*), made in a mould
found at the abbey (**29a**). This was a high-
quality mould, made from imported
lithographic limestone. Inns and hostelries
would also have offered accommodation, *en
route*, and in Whithorn itself.

In 1427 James I issued a general safe conduct
to all pilgrims from England and the Isle of Man
specifying conditions they had to follow: 'they
were to come by sea or land and to return by
the same route, to bear themselves as pilgrims
and to remain in Scotland no more than 15
days; they were to wear openly one badge as
they came, and another (to be received from the
prior of Whithorn) on their return journey'. One
such small, cast-lead badge showing St Ninian
in bishop's vestments, and dated to between the
thirteenth and fifteenth centuries, was found
during the excavations (**29b**). This was pierced
for attaching to clothing, and features the saint
with a pair of shackles, a regular attribute of
Ninian who was renowned as a liberator of
Christian prisoners. The accounts of James IV's
pilgrimages show that he spent quite large sums
on badges; in July 1504 he spent 4 shillings on
signacula, and 9 shillings on these tokens in the
following year. At continental shrines the

production of badges was strictly controlled by the church which housed the shrine, and which received a significant royalty on sales. A pilgrims' badge from St Peter's, Rome was also found in the excavations.

Pilgrims travelling by sea from Ireland and Man would have arrived at various ports and landings. The chapel at Mochrum dedicated to St Finnian was erected on the shore at one such landing place 19 km (11.8 miles) north-west of Whithorn, the surviving fabric dates from the tenth century. The principal port for pilgrims was at the Isle of Whithorn, 5 km (3 miles) south-east of the shrine. A small chapel was provided here for pilgrims to give immediate thanks for their safe arrival. The standing structure probably dates to around 1300, replacing an earlier chapel.

The experience of the pilgrim at Whithorn in later medieval times

It is possible to reconstruct the stations of pilgrimage on a feast day at the cathedral when all the major relics would have been displayed (**20** and **21**). Having arrived safely in the town, the pilgrims would have processed from the priory gatehouse located at the west end of the high street of the medieval burgh. The impressive stone gateway formed the interface between the profane life of the town and the sacred space of the monastic enclosure and burial ground. The pilgrims entered the nave of the church through the south door, and were quickly rewarded with their first contact with a relic of St Ninian displayed on an altar close to the crossing screen. This is the altar in the 'uter kirk' where James IV made an offering during his pilgrimage in March 1508. James made offerings at each station, including 'the chapel on the hill', which has not been located. The pilgrims were then privileged to pass through the screen and to follow the well-worn route, possibly passing between the north transept, and the choir and high altar, which were screened off so as not to interfere with the canons' worship. With rising excitement the pilgrims

were then brought into direct contact with the main shrine in the feretory chapel behind the high altar. The chapel would have been richly fitted out with carved and painted decoration, including some of the precious gifts from beneficiaries of Ninianic miracles, such as the Frenchman who gifted a silver ship to the shrine in 1434 in thanksgiving for his salvation through prayer to the saint during a storm at sea. Statues of the saint would have graced the church, and what appears to be one of these, executed in oak, was found in a bog near the priory where it had been thrown by the reforming iconoclasts (**22**). This statue was no more than 1 m (3.3 ft) tall when complete, and would have been ideal for use in the processions, inside the church and around the town, which were an integral part of the rituals. No trace of the shrine has survived, although we can assume that it was another highly decorated, church-shaped wooden *chasse*, covered with precious metals, as postulated at Glasgow, replacing the ancient stone sarcophagus described in the *Miracula*. Some of the pilgrims may have been permitted direct contact with relics for healing purposes, producing a tremendously heightened atmosphere of awe and wonder, especially when this resulted in immediate miraculous cures.

In processing around the east end of the relic chapel, the pilgrims then encountered the altar of the Virgin, another very holy station. A large southern chapel was added during a major rebuilding and restoration programme, which took place around 1500, with indulgences provided in return for offerings. This chapel provided space for further devotional altars as well, and created a grander setting in which pilgrims could observe the activity around the main shrine.

The dramatic effect was further increased as the pilgrims then descended into the crypt containing the empty tomb, located directly beneath the feretory (**23**). This small barrel-vaulted space can still be visited, although the effect is less impressive than when it was

20 A speculative reconstruction of the two-storey east end of Whithorn in the
later medieval period. The cover has been removed from the shrine in the relic
chapel, where the walls are decorated with biblical scenes, and where relic
cupboards and statues of the saint can be seen. Pilgrims are passing between
the shrine and the tomb in the crypt. (Drawn by David Simon.)

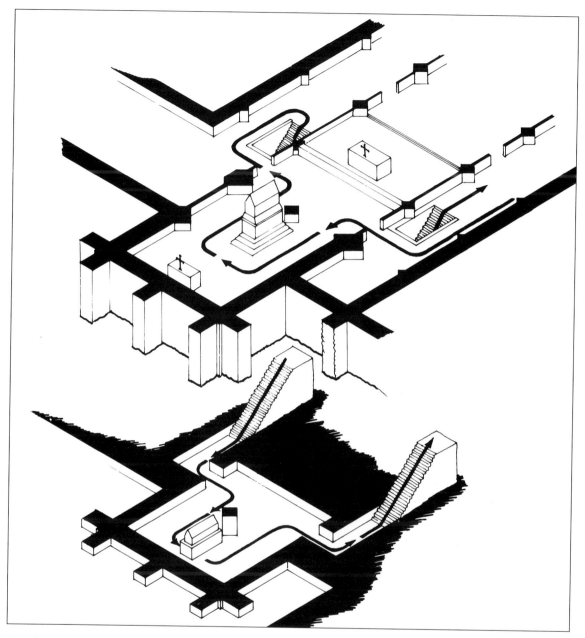

21 Schematic floor plans of Whithorn, showing ambulatory routes.

originally roofed with a ribbed vault which rested on a central pier. At such busy times a one-way system would have operated, and the lesser officials of the cathedral would have stewarded the faithful out of the very confined space of the crypt up and out by another stair to the north. From here, the pilgrims could either go around the main shrine again and then back to the nave by the southern transept, or else they could retrace their steps to the nave by the way they had come in.

St Ninian's Cave

The remains of a collapsed cave believed to be Ninian's *deserta* (hermitage) stands on the shore near the mouth of the verdant and atmospheric Physgill Glen, 5 km (3 miles) south-west of

22 Oak statue of a bishop, possibly St Ninian, found in a bog close to the priory. Fifteenth-century, 0.83 m (3 ft) in height.

Whithorn (**24**). Excavations here in the nineteenth century cleared debris from the cave and uncovered a number of carved stones dated to between the eighth and eleventh century. Votive crosses carved on the walls by medieval pilgrims can still be seen, along with the evidence of continuing devotion in modern times. The cave was featured in the *Miracula* poem: 'Ninian studied heavenly wisdom with a devoted mind in a cave of horrible blackness'.

The relics of St Ninian and the healing cult

During the early centuries of the cult, the relics consisted of a full set of bones, along with secondary relics, including the saint's clothing, his staff, bell, and psalm book. Over a period of more than 1000 years, the bones became dispersed, and those which remained suffered deterioration from handling and general decay. By the time of James IV, it is probable that only a few bones survived, most notably arm bones which he ordered the royal goldsmith to enshrine in a new silver gilt reliquary. James also provided a new reliquary made from 25 ounces of silver, gold and precious stones for another group of bones in 1506. The arm reliquary survived the Reformation, and by the early seventeenth century was in the safekeeping of the Scots seminary at Douai in northern France, along with the head shrine of St Margaret. Sadly, these relics did not survive the French Revolution. Other objects which adorned the shrine were also attributed miraculous powers. There was a famous painting of the saint which was removed by the Scots in advance of a pilgrimage by Prince Edward (later Edward II) in 1301 whilst on campaign, either as an act of spite or to protect the image from looting. Even though the painting had been taken some 80 km (50 miles) away to Sweetheart Abbey, it had returned unaided the next morning.

The cult of St Ninian is unusual in that from the time of the earliest records on, it was clearly established as a cult primarily associated with healing by direct contiguity with the relics of the

23 The crypt at Whithorn, with the twin barrel vaults of about 1500 which replaced the original rib vaulting.

24 St Ninian's Cave from an engraving by Sir Herbert Maxwell.

saint. The *Miracula* and later documents describe miracles of healing including healing of paralysis, leprosy and blindness. These cures were wrought by various means involving the tomb, the relics, soil (presumably dust from the holy places), the saint's clothing, water recovered from washing the bones, and a lost holy spring or cistern, along with solitary nocturnal vigils at the shrine or tomb. Cures of leprosy attracted King Robert I (1306–29) to endure a long and painful journey to Whithorn in 1329, just three months before his death.

The large numbers of sick people seeking cures would have been provided with special facilities at the monastery, including an infirmary and trained medical practitioners. Evidence of medicinal herbs and a possible surgeon's knife were found in the excavations from the

25 Reconstruction of Whithorn Priory during the rebuilding of around 1500. Pilgrims, including James IV, might have bought their badges from the stalls on the street leading up to the church.

Northumbrian period. Although 1600 of the many thousands of graves were investigated, the range and proportion of chronic illness was found to be no more than the average observed in other excavated medieval cemeteries. While it can be safely assumed that pilgrims who died at the goal of their pilgrimage were buried in the cemetery, it is almost impossible to identify these because of the rapidity of death caused by diseases and infection in medieval times, leaving no trace on the bones.

Galloway was a traditionally independent province which had long resisted integration with the medieval kingdom, although this was effectively achieved by the fourteenth century. The Crown had persistently adopted and revered the cult of St Ninian, and the personal pilgrimages of the later Stewart Kings certainly aided the process of reconciliation. By the time the *Aberdeen Breviary* was printed in 1510, St Ninian was at the height of his popularity, and the subject of national devotion to rival that of St Andrew (**25**).

St Cuthbert and St Waltheof of Melrose

A monastery was founded at Old Melrose on the Tweed in the middle of the seventh century. The old Cumbric place-name, Melrose, means 'bare promontory', and this conjures up the remote, desired setting, washed by the river on three sides and embanked on the other, sought by Aidan and his monks from Iona, when they colonized the site from Lindisfarne. Cuthbert, the son of a local Anglian farmer, entered the monastery at Old Melrose in 651 having had a vision of St Aidan. The monastery was destroyed by the Scots in 839, but some kind of religious house was in existence here again by the later eleventh century, after the site was recolonized by Turgot in about 1075. David I invited the Cistercians of Rievaulx to build their monastery here at the place sanctified by St Cuthbert, but they preferred the site 4 km (2.5 miles) to the west, taking the place-name with them. A chapel at Old Melrose continued to function as a place of pilgrimage. In 1322, Symon, Bishop of Galloway offered an indulgence of 40 days off purgatory to pilgrims to the chapel of St Cuthbert, to raise funds to enable rebuilding following damage caused by the English. In 1437, a monk of Melrose Abbey named John travelled to Rome to secure an indulgence from the Pope for pilgrims who visited the chapel on the feast days of the saint. The site is now viewed unknowingly by thousands each year, as it is located in the foreground of Scott's View, a romantic vista made famous by the nineteenth-century novelist Sir Walter Scott (**colour plate 2**).

Waltheof was the stepson of David I, and had therefore given up more than most to become a monk. In 1148 he became the second Abbot of the Cistercian monastery at Melrose (**26**). He died in 1159 and was buried at a spot he himself had chosen close to the entrance of the chapter house. He was honoured as a saint after his death, presumably because of the great piety he had exhibited in life, coupled with miracles

26 The east end of Melrose Abbey.

wrought at his tomb in death. The medieval *Melrose Chronicle* tells of cures affected by placing the afflicted part of the body next to the same part of the sculpted effigy of the saint. As part of the process of sanctification, Waltheof's tomb was opened during a ceremony led by Abbot Jocelin (see page 18), at which time the body was found to be incorrupt, a sure sign of sanctity. When Jocelin became Bishop of Glasgow (1174–99), head of the diocese which contained Melrose, he carried on the campaign to canonize Waltheof. This process was continued after Jocelin's death, when the same monk who had produced a new *Life of St Kentigern* was commissioned to write a promotional *Life of St Waltheof*. The tomb was opened again in 1240, when only bones were found. A few small relics were removed at this time, from which 'sick people gained many benefits'.

It is difficult to know how significant this cult was, and to what extent Melrose Abbey was a place of pilgrimage. An exciting clue, however, was discovered during the clearing of debris from the site in the 1920s, when fragments of a tomb-shrine were uncovered, apparently in the vicinity of the chapter house (27 and 28). These pieces, along with the possible fragments found at Glasgow Cathedral (12), represent the only surviving tomb-shrines of later medieval saints to survive the Reformation. The Melrose fragments have been reconstructed to form one end of a tomb chest of local stone, the surfaces of which were overlain with gesso and gilding, to produce a highly ornate effect. The shrine may have been provided with apertures through which the devotees could touch the relics. The nature of the inter-war clearance excavations which produced the tomb fragments, were somewhat imprecise, and there is no certainty regarding the find-spot. The chapter house at Melrose is also reputed to have been a royal shrine, housing the heart of King Robert I, which was taken on crusade against the Moors in Spain. The heart was returned to Scotland, and interred within the abbey by the middle of the fourteenth century. It does seem likely that this relic, as well as the bones of Waltheof, was the subject of popular devotion, and yet it is difficult to imagine how this could have been managed if both were interred within the chapter house, normally an exclusively private monastic building. Indeed, the contemplative life desired by the Cistercians was disrupted by the expressions of popular devotion at the shrine soon after Waltheof's death, to the extent that public access to the chapter house was banned.

The abbey church could certainly have accommodated pilgrims, and it would have been possible for relic shrines and altars to have been erected at the east end, possibly during the great rebuilding here in the thirteenth century. There is also the strong possibility that a relic of St Cuthbert was housed here, bearing in mind the close connection between Melrose and that saint. King Robert I was a devotee of St Cuthbert, which explains his instruction to have his heart enshrined here – beside shrines of Cuthbert and Waltheof? What may well be a Melrose pilgrims' badge can be found in the collections of the National Museums of Scotland (29c). This badge displays a punning device which spells out the later medieval misinterpretation of the place-name *Melros*, represented by a mason's hammer (*mel*), and a rose (*ros*), the latter being a symbol associated with the Cistercians. This might also be held up as evidence of popular pilgrimage, which could only have been permitted within the usual location, that is in a feretory chapel behind the high altar. If this were so, then the lead container excavated in the chapter house in 1996 is unlikely to contain Bruce's heart, unless this had been removed from the east end of the church.

The Cross Kirk of Peebles

A chance discovery in the thirteenth century led to the establishment of a major pilgrimage church at Peebles. The fourteenth-century chronicler Fordun tells of the miraculous discovery of 'a stately and venerable cross',

27 Possible fragments of St Waltheof's tomb-shrine, from Melrose Abbey, reconstructed to form one end of the tomb with a central aperture, backed by an internal support. This would originally have been gilded and decorated to produce a highly ornate finish.

28 Reconstruction drawing of St Waltheof's tomb, which would have been about 2 m (6.6 ft) in length.

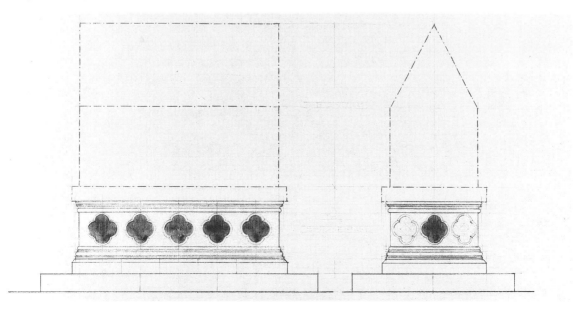

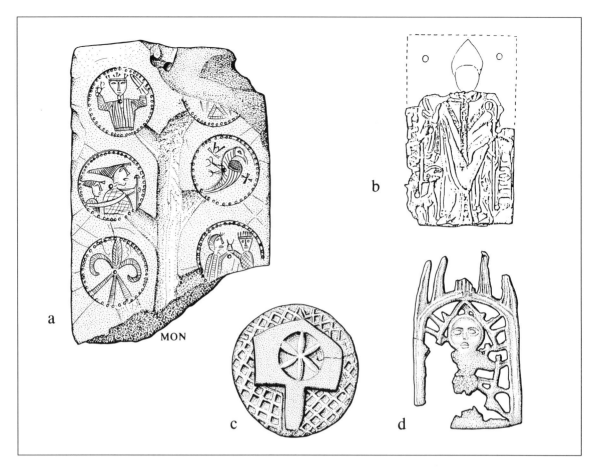

29 a. Badge mould from Dundrennan Abbey made of imported lithographic limestone b. Late medieval tin alloy badge from Whithorn, probably depicting St Ninian c. Badge from Melrose Abbey, with a mason's mel and a rose spelling out the place-name d. Fifteenth-century tin alloy badge found at Fast Castle, Berwickshire, depicting the Assumption of the Virgin. A possible source for this badge might have been the Whitekirk shrine (Actual size. Drawn by Marion O'Neil, except b.)

found in May 1261 in the presence of Alexander III, along with various good men, priests, clerics, and burgesses. It was found resting on an inscribed stone, now believed to have read 'the place of St Ninian the Bishop', which might indicate that the cross was buried within the remains of an ancient church, possibly founded from Whithorn in the seventh century. The slab was next to skeletal remains interred within what we would interpret today as a Bronze Age short cist, although when found in the thirteenth century, it was believed to be an early Christian burial associated with the slab. The circumstances of discovery would seem to be somewhat orchestrated, as the King would not have been on hand every day, but nevertheless there was a firm belief that this wonderful object contained a piece of the True Cross.

Alexander III endowed the construction of a fine church, which incorporated an unusual shrine in the south wall, with an arched aperture which enabled pilgrims to view the sacred slab and associated cist from both inside and outside the building (30). The remains of this shrine can still be seen, close to the screen between nave and chancel. Once pilgrims had made their devotions here, they would have come to the high altar where the magnificent cross was displayed. Fordun records that 'many miracles were worked

through the cross, and crowds of people do flock there making their gifts and vows to God'. At some time, the administration of the church was gifted to the Trinitarian friars, who were often associated with pilgrimage places, as appropriate to their origin as an order which raised funds to ransom Christian captives in the Holy Land. It was not until 1474 that conventual status was achieved under the patronage of James III, at which time the construction of a cloister was begun to the north of the church so as not to enclose the shrine in the south wall. James IV perpetuated the royal patronage of the Cross Kirk, which was included in his annual round of pilgrimages. The Treasurer's Accounts record his offerings at the shrine, as well as various generous gifts of precious metals to embellish the relics. In 1507 he had the royal goldsmith make a cross-shaped reliquary of pure gold to enshrine the relic. This patronage was continued by James V.

30 Reconstruction of the Trinitarian convent of Cross Kirk, Peebles in the late fifteenth century. The shrine can be seen in the south wall; this was unusual, and allowed the pilgrims to view the shrine from both inside and outside the church.

Two hospitals dedicated to St Leonard were established close by to serve as pilgrims' hostels, with one in Peebles itself, and other 3 km (1.9 miles) east on the Tweed at Eshiels. The busiest times would have been at the two feasts: one celebrating the finding of the Cross in May, and the Feast of the Exaltation of the Cross in August.

St Baldred of the Bass Rock

Baldred is reputed to have been a priest or monk of Lindisfarne, who was sent to minister to the Anglian people of East Lothian in the mid eighth century. He is believed to have had a monastery at Tyninghame, where the ruins of the later Romanesque parish church now stand in parkland beside Tyninghame House. Two places of retreat are associated with him, the most famous being the Bass Rock, which he shared with the solan geese and cormorants, where his cell was incorporated into the later medieval church (**31**). A cave bears his name at Seacliff Beach; this was investigated in the nineteenth century when an altar and human burials were found. Close by the cave is a rock formation known as 'St Baldred's Boat', being the remains of the stone vessel which, legend has it, brought him to these shores.

Another part of his legend recounts the problems which arose at his death in 756, when his three churches in this neighbourhood fought for possession of his corpse. The saint solved this problem by the miraculous triplication of his body, allowing the churches at Tyninghame, Auldhame, and Prestonkirk to each possess his

relics. The cult was very localized, although the fact that he was held in great reverence throughout the medieval period is indicated by the number of places which bear his name. St Baldred's Well can still be seen by the River Tyne 50 m (165 ft) east of the church at Prestonkirk. Until recently, the well was 'famed for its cold purity and healing qualities'. His festival was celebrated on 6 March.

Whitekirk and the Holy Well of Our Lady

In the later medieval period Baldred's cult was overshadowed by the magnification of another of his churches as a major pilgrimage resort, at Whitekirk, only 1.5 km (1 mile) north-west of his monastery at Tyninghame. The curative powers of the well dedicated to Our Lady, situated 200 m (220 yds) to the east of the church, brought fame to Whitekirk at some time in the thirteenth century. In 1309, John Abernethy, possibly in thanksgiving for a cure, received permission with the help of the Cistercians of Melrose to erect a shrine dedicated to the Holy Mother in the church.

31 St Baldred's chapel on the Bass Rock, standing above the late medieval fortifications, in an engraving of the 1690s by Captain John Slezer.

The church was pillaged by Edward III's troops during their invasion of the Lothians in 1338, when they sailed up the Tyne and stripped the shrine of its rich offerings. This sacrilege did not pass unpunished however, as one soldier was killed by a falling crucifix, and the others all drowned when departing the mouth of the Tyne. The fame of the church as a place of pilgrimage continued to grow, with papal indulgences offered to those 'who gave alms to the fabric of the church'.

The most famous Whitekirk pilgrim was a certain Italian diplomat named Piccolomini, later to become Pope Pius II, who was shipwrecked near Dunbar while on a mission to Scotland in December 1435. To give thanks for being saved he executed his vow to walk barefoot through the snow to the nearest shrine dedicated to Our Lady, which was 12 km (7.4 miles) distant at Whitekirk. At around the same time, James I is credited with building a number of guest-houses near the church to accommodate the increasing numbers of pilgrims. Recent excavations have identified the possible remains of some of these close to the church barn to the north of Whitekirk. Another hostel or priest's house may have stood just to the east of the church, where two large eighteenth-century tombstones are supported by fragments of older walling. An exciting discovery was made during the recent renovation of the barn, when fragments of a shrine or altar, decorated with the Cistercian rose motif and an encircled cross, were found. It is even possible that this was part of the shrine dedicated in 1309, and broken up as building stone at the Reformation. Further archaeological work has confirmed that the no longer visible site of the well is as marked on Ordnance Survey maps. It is not known whether a separate chapel stood here, although this is quite possible. Healing rituals would have taken place at the well, and pilgrims would have been given the holy water to take away in return for their offerings.

The shrine benefited from being close to Edinburgh, from where it could be reached in a vigorous day-trip on horseback. James IV was a regular attender, sometimes taking lodgings in the guest-houses, and partaking of cards and other entertainments during his short stay. No badge or token has ever been directly associated with this pilgrimage, although it is possible that a fifteenth-century badge depicting the Assumption of the Virgin Mary, found at Fast Castle on the Berwickshire coast east of Whitekirk, may have originated from the East Lothian shrine (**29d**).

The Loretto Chapel at Musselburgh

This cult was based on the belief that the Virgin Mary's house in Nazareth had been miraculously transported by angels to Loretto in Italy in 1295. Enthusiasm for this cult was revitalized throughout Europe in 1507 when the *Santa Casa* was formally approved by the Pope, resulting in a number of such houses being built in imitation. The Scots were not to be left out, and Loretto chapels were built at Perth in 1528, and just outside the east gate of Musselburgh around 1533. These could only be constructed having first obtained a stone from Loretto upon which the Angel Gabriel had stood.

Although both were supported by James V, we know little of the *Santa Casa* of Perth. In August 1536, James V made a barefoot pilgrimage from Linlithgow Palace to the chapel at Musselburgh, before voyaging to France to enter into his short-lived marriage to the Princess Madeleine. At this time he made offerings which were accepted by the hermit who cared for the chapel and holy well. The shrine was later to be mocked by Sir David Lindsay due to 'the immorality of the pilgrims and the bogus miracles'.

St Triduana of Restalrig

Hidden away among housing estates on the east side of Edinburgh is one of the most remarkable and now rarely visited reliquary chapels. This was reputed to be the burial-place of Triduana, one of whose legends places her among the virgins who accompanied St Rule to Scotland with the Andrean relics. While in Angus, so the

32 St Triduana's well-shrine in the lower part of the fifteenth-century, hexagonal, royal chapel, now located to the east of central Edinburgh.

legend has it, she responded to the unwelcome advances of a Pictish chieftain by plucking out her eyes and sending them to him skewered on thorns. A cult grew up around her at a number of holy wells and springs, including Papa Westray (see page 99), and all dedicated to the healing of eye complaints. This is a good example of the Christian adoption of pagan devotion to water spirits.

The Restalrig shrine benefited from the late medieval revival of interest in pilgrimage, and by around 1486 James III granted the church collegiate status, with seven or eight priests to say masses for their King. There was a swing away from endowing monasteries at this time, in favour of creating collegiate churches, so-called because a college of priests would be established with the primary function of praying for the souls of the founding family. The relics of St Triduana were enshrined in a newly constructed, two-storey hexagonal chapel, described by Pope Innocent VIII as 'a sumptuous new work'. The papal legate had been taken to see this King's Chapel by James, to show that Scotland could create reliquary chapels to rival those anywhere in Christendom (32). The upper part of the chapel has gone, but this would have been lit by large traceried windows with the altar and feretory at the east end. To visit the holy spring in the lower floor must have been an extraordinary experience; the floor of the beautiful rib-vaulted interior was constantly awash with water from Triduana's spring, and thronged with visually impaired pilgrims and their supporters. Blindness would have been a common disability, often simply resulting from severe vitamin deficiency in the poor diet of medieval Scots.

4
Fife: the pilgrim's kingdom

The shrine of St Andrew, in the medieval city which took his name, was in the first rank of pilgrimage places, where pilgrims could come into contact with relics of a martyred apostle of Christ, brother of St Peter the father of the Church. There were only two places where this was possible in western Christendom, here, and at the shrine of St James the Greater at Compostela. It is fair to say, however, that St Andrews never achieved the popularity of Santiago.

The medieval pilgrims believed a foundation legend which entailed the relics being carried from Andrew's burial-place at Patras in Greece by a monk named Regulus (Rule), who had been instructed to do so in a vision. These were later miraculously discovered, and churches built at this specially chosen spot which became St Andrews. The reality is probably somewhat different: the promontory where the cathedral now stands was named *Kinrymont*, meaning 'the end of the king's muir', which was probably a Pictish royal administrative centre, pre-dating the arrival of the relics. The cult might have been introduced from Northumbria by Bishop Acca of Hexham, during the reign of Angus I (730–61), to a site which already contained one or more churches and well-established Christian cemeteries (**colour plate 3**). Acca was a renowned collector of relics, and when he fled to Pictland to escape the wrath of his King, he may well have arrived with relics of St Andrew who was currently very popular with the Saxons. The relics may have been acquired in Rome by Bishop

Wilfred, Acca's predecessor. Angus' own position was clearly enhanced by being associated with an apostle, who, legend has it, appeared to him in a dream to promise victory in battle.

The strength of the cult continued to grow at Kinrymont, attracting pilgrims to what must have resembled an Irish type of monastic enclosure, adjacent to a royal residence, with as many as seven churches and chapels referred to in the early documents. The enclosure would have been smaller than the later walled precinct, with high cliffs to north and east, above the harbour, and bounded by what is now Pends Road to the south. A secular settlement grew up to the west of the enclosure, located at the east end of North Street, and possibly taking up part of the land now occupied by the ruined cathedral. Initially, this was a local cult, and it was not until c 906 that Kinrymont became the chief focus of national religious activity and the seat of the high bishop, taking over the role previously centred on Abernethy and Dunkeld. The first record of this being an important place of pilgrimage is a reference in a contemporary chronicle to the death of an Irish prince here, while on pilgrimage in 967.

The first pilgrims would have visited relics in a number of the churches on the promontory, some of which were in a line west to east, culminating with a church on the cliff site now occupied by St Mary's. Excavations here revealed a cemetery in use from the fifth to the twelfth century. The main church would have

been in the western part of the site, close to the east end of the later cathedral, as indicated by the cross-shafts and other early stones found here. The most famous and extraordinary find from this location was the St Andrews' sarcophagus, a beautifully carved tomb-shrine dated to the early ninth century (**33**). Pilgrims to this lost church would have seen this tomb standing to the left of the high altar, end-on to the viewer. The sarcophagus is decorated with powerful Old Testament iconography featuring David, the good and just King, indicating that this stone coffin was made to contain the relics of a Pictish King, possibly Constantine, son of Fergus, who died in 820, and who may have been regarded as a saint. Indeed, this reliquary may have been the main focus of devotion in early medieval times, as it has been suggested that the existence of the Andrean relics was a political invention of the eleventh century. Whatever the truth was, there can be no doubt that the *Basilica Sancti Andree apostoli* was established as a famous place of pilgrimage by at least this time.

Queen Margaret and St Andrews

By the time of Queen Margaret (1070–93), the pilgrimage was popular enough to warrant her endowing the free crossing of the Forth west of

33 The St Andrews' sarcophagus, side panel and corner slabs, approximately 1.75 m (6 ft) in length. This beautifully carved tomb-shrine dates from the early ninth century, when it would have stood end-on to the worshippers to the left of the high altar, in a now lost church which once stood in the vicinity of St Andrews Cathedral. (Drawn by Ian G. Scott.)

Edinburgh. She supported the churches at St Andrews, where she would have been a frequent visitor, and provided at least one precious adornment, a jewelled cross which graced the high altar of the principal church. Margaret may have helped Fothad, who was probably the last native Gaelic-speaking Bishop, to build the church we now know as St Rule's. This was the first cathedral dedicated to St Andrew, initially comprising a nave and the very high tower which has acted as a beacon for pilgrims ever since. The focus of this church was the *Mòr Breac*, a Celtic reliquary, maybe a jewelled box or another house shrine like the Monymusk reliquary, which contained the relics, believed to be a tooth, a kneecap, three fingers of the right hand, and an arm bone. This box was light enough to be carried in procession, and was still in use in the thirteenth century.

The Hospital of St Andrew and St Leonard

The main pilgrims' hostel was probably in existence by Margaret's time, located in an outer enclosure south-west of Kinrymont, 200 m (220 yds) distant from the early cathedral. This was a possession of the Culdee clergy who were responsible for much of the worship here. The Culdees were a community of monks who lived under a rule which originated in Ireland. During the reign of Alexander I (1107–24) the hospital could accommodate six pilgrims, and it retained this function until the sixteenth century, as well as serving as the almonry for the Augustinian priory (34). No doubt only the poorest and feeblest pilgrims found accommodation at the hostel, while others found shelter at inns or with the non-monastic officials of the cathedral. By around 1200, the hospital's church was elevated to serve the small parish of St Leonard's, to alleviate pressure on the main parish church of Holy Trinity, which until 1412 was located in the monastic precinct, between the old and the new cathedrals.

The arrival of the Augustinians

St Andrews was transformed into a newly founded house of Augustinian canons when Bishop Robert was appointed by Alexander I in the last year of his reign. The Bishop inherited the existing cathedral (St Rule's) and transformed this to better suit the reformed liturgy, by adding a new nave to the west, and by enlarging the east end. The arched opening running through the building would have enabled pilgrims to have a view of the shrine behind the high altar, which may have been raised up.

The old church was clearly unsuitable and soon after 1160 work had started on laying out the foundations of a great new cathedral, which required enormous investment and foresight, with the main phase of construction lasting over 150 years. The continuing promotion of the cult was now of even greater importance, to help maximize revenues needed to fund the building works. The east end, housing the high altar and possibly the relic chapel were the first parts to be completed, possibly around 1230 when the church was in partial use, so as to enable the canons' worship and the installation of the relics in their glorious new setting. Veneration of the relics would have been an uncomfortable, if not dangerous experience, as throughout this period the church and cloister was a building site with precarious timber scaffolds, and stone being winched up to the heights.

Patron saint

Up until the end of the eleventh century, the saint who could claim to have the widest following was Columba. But it was St Andrew who was honoured as the patron saint from then on, the reason for this being, as expressed by the historian Dr Simon Taylor, that 'only the first-chosen Apostle could stand up to the bullying metropolitan claims of St Peter of York'. In other words, the patronage of St Andrew was a powerful shield to be used by the Scots' Crown and Church to counter the claims of overlordship, secular and religious, from England. The cult received its greatest boost in the later thirteenth century at the time of the descent into decades of war with the English. St Andrew became recognized as patron and protector, with his relics being the physical manifestation of that protection extended to the Scots, his chosen people. So it was not surprising that building works at the cathedral were hurriedly completed four years after victory at Bannockburn in 1314, with endowments presented in thanksgiving, allowing a splendid consecration to take place in the presence of King Robert I in July 1318.

Routes to St Andrews

The four principal routes into Fife each involved a crossing of the Forth or Tay, either to east or west (35). A complex network of ferries, roads, bridges, chapels, hospitals, and inns was created and maintained to ease the way for the pilgrims to the national shrine, the support of this infrastructure being a recognized act of piety.

34 An old photograph showing the rare survival of the lay-out of a medieval hospital – St Mary's, Winchester. The chapel was at the far end, while the poor and sick were cared for in the aisles to left and right. Some of the pilgrims' hospices in Scotland would have taken this form.

Pilgrims coming from the north-west, including those travelling from the important town of Perth and great abbey at Scone, took a ferry across the Tay at its confluence with the River Earn. They travelled east past Macduff's Cross, an ancient marker on the western boundary of the lands of the Earls of Fife, and where an oratory may have stood. This route can still be followed from here to Gallows Hill, and on to Grange of Lindores, the home farm of the nearby abbey, where alms and shelter could

be found (**36**). The route continued on the higher ground to the parish church of the Holy Trinity of Moonzie, on a hilltop where pilgrims might have had their first glimpse of the distant spires of their goal. The income of the church at Moonzie was gifted by Prior Henry of St Andrews to the Trinitarians of Scotlandwell in the early thirteenth century, and it is possible that this was to support another hospice here on the pilgrims' route. The pilgrims would have continued east from Moonzie, possibly bypassing Cupar to the north, going by Pitbladdo and Foodieash, before crossing the Eden near Dairsie Castle, and then heading to St Andrews via Strathkinness. It is important to

35 Pilgrims' ferries and routes to St Andrews. The distance from Queensferry to Scotlandwell is 24 km (15 miles).

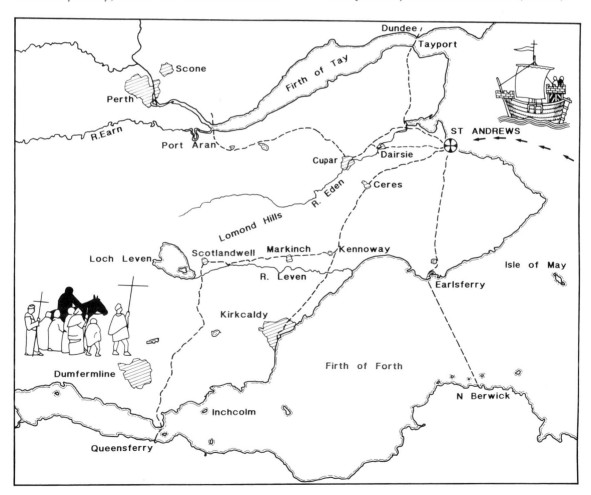

36 A 'green road' preserved in the landscape above
Newburgh in north-west Fife, which marks the probable
pilgrimage route from Perth and Scone. Over the hill in
the distance was the Grange (monastic farm) of
Lindores Abbey where pilgrims would be given alms.

remember that during the medieval period, some of the lower lying routes in use today were not suitable as this land was boggy and impassable, hence the necessity to keep to the higher ground.

Before Bishop Wardlaw had the stone bridge built at Guardbridge in 1419, pilgrims coming from west or north had to cross the the tidal River Eden by ford or ferry, which could be dangerous (37). Around this time a group of 20 high-ranking monks and clerics were drowned while crossing, and this may have prompted the bridge works. The route from the north to St Andrews involved a ferry crossing of the Tay, which was administered by the canons of the priory, disembarking at Portincrag (Tayport),

where a hospice is recorded. Pilgrims from Dundee would have had the option of crossing directly from there to Woodhaven on the Fife shore. The route south passed the old parish church at Forgan, then onto Vicarsford and Leuchars, and we know that at least part of this was a cobbled road, referred to in a fourteenth-century charter as the 'ancient royal highway'. Before the bridge was built, pilgrims were probably ferried across the Eden from Coble Point. The derivation of the Guardbridge place-name, cognate with the French *gare*, shows that this was a *statio* or meeting-place, provided with a hostel where pilgrims banded together before making their triumphant approach to St Andrews over the last few kilometres of their journey.

The most famous route was the Queen's Ferry across the Forth, used by pilgrims from Edinburgh and the south-west. Queen Margaret's biographer, Turgot, writing shortly after her death in 1093, recorded that not only did she provide ships for the crossing, but that Margaret also endowed hostels on either side of the Forth, which she provided with staff who were 'to wait upon them (the pilgrims) with great care'. From here the road headed north via Crossgates and Lochore to the east end of Loch Leven, where there was a hospital with an ancient and famous healing well, of such importance to have determined the place-name, Scotlandwell. This was a long-established route, referred to in an eleventh-century charter of King Macbeth as 'the public causeway which leads to Inverkeithing', just to the north of North Queensferry, 24 km (15 miles) from Scotlandwell. This route was important enough to have been provided with a bridge over the River Leven, first mentioned in the early thirteenth century. In the twelfth century the hospital was under the direct control of the Bishops of St Andrews, and was dedicated to St Thomas Becket after his death in 1172. In the thirteenth century the hospital was made part of a house of Trinitarians. Here pilgrims were accommodated, and the sick were cared for; King Robert I issued a number of charters from

37 Guardbridge just to the west of St Andrews: the fifteenth-century bridge is located between the modern road and the base of the old railway bridge.

Scotlandwell, recording his presence when he was presumably seeking a cure for his leprosy. Inverkeithing harbour and burgh continued to play an important part in the management of pilgrimage traffic in the later medieval period. The large guest range at the Franciscan friary in the centre of Inverkeithing, which can still be seen, would have provided comfortable accommodation for those passing through.

The route east from here kept to the high ground in the Leven valley, past Markinch and Kennoway, where the road joined with the coastal route from Kirkcaldy, before heading north-east towards Ceres. A fourteenth-century charter records the location of the 'Pilgrim Gait' (road) in the vicinity of Pratis, just a few kilometres to the north of Kennoway. From Ceres the pilgrims followed the Bishop's Road to St Andrews via Blebo.

The Queen's Ferry was matched in the eastern part of the Forth by the Earl's Ferry, endowed by the Earls of Fife, which carried pilgrims from North Berwick to the port of Earlsferry, by Elie. This crossing was established in the mid twelfth century by Earl Duncan, who also endowed a pilgrims' hospice at North Berwick (38). The economics of pilgrimage was responsible for the growth of both settlements at either end of the crossing. A house of Cistercian nuns was founded at North Berwick in the mid twelfth century. The nuns were responsible for managing both sides of the crossing, including the parish church of St Andrews and the hospice which both stood by the harbour. Pilgrims could worship here before embarking, and could also purchase their St Andrews', and other, pilgrims' badges. A mould for casting these, dated to the thirteenth to fourteenth century was found at the church in the nineteenth century (**39d**). A similar mould was found at Kinross, to the south of Perth (**39e**). These were fairly coarse products compared to the badge found during recent excavations near St Andrews Castle (**39c**). It is likely that the nuns of North Berwick controlled the manufacture and sale of these highly prized souvenirs, which were probably also made at other places on the main routes to the shrine (**39a**). A different type of St Andrews' badge is believed to have been obtained at the shrine, to be worn on the return journey. The most distant discovery of one of these badges was from London (**39b**). Pilgrims *en route* to the ferry would also have been accommodated by the Trinitarians at Dunbar, just to the east of North Berwick.

The nuns ran hospitals for the pilgrims on both sides of the Forth, and the remains of the chapel which stood near the Earlsferry hospital

38 North Berwick harbour, with the site of St Andrew's church and the pilgrims' hospice in the central grassy area.

39 St Andrews' pilgrims' badges and moulds, thirteenth- to fifteenth-century: a. Tin alloy badge found in Perth b. Tin alloy badge found in London c. Lead alloy badge found in St Andrews d. Stone mould for casting badges from North Berwick e. Stone mould from Kinross. (Actual size. Drawn by Marion O'Neil.)

40 Speculative reconstruction of the translation of the relics of St Ethernan, into the mortuary chapel built in the ninth to tenth century on the Isle of May, Fife. (Drawn by Alan Braby.)

can still be seen. This settlement is now merged with Elie, a place-name which may be derived from the Gaelic *Ealadh*, which means tomb or burial-place, possibly a name given to a place where the corpses of important people were landed *en route* to St Andrews for burial. Those who were brave enough to 'tempt the stormy Frith' endured a crossing of 32 km (20 miles); one or more purpose-built ferry boats may have served this route, although at busy festival times any small vessel of the coastal trade would have been pressed into service. Once the pilgrims had arrived on the Fife shore, they had to travel a further 35 km (22 miles) north to St Andrews, passing by the nuns' grange farm as they left Earlsferry behind. This same route was taken by King Edward I in March 1304, when he rode along the coast to near Earlsferry, before heading north to St Andrews via Kincaple. The ferry was still in existence after the Reformation, and an account survives of a particularly awful crossing endured in 1585 by James Melville, a professor at St Andrews University, when travelling with his young family and other companions in a coal boat.

Saints and the Forth islands

Water-borne transport, in favourable weather, was by far the quickest and easiest means of travel in the medieval period. The Forth was an especially busy waterway at this time, offering easy access to centres of power, prestige and population, for a wide range of purposes, ranging from religious conversion through to trade and diplomacy. A major increase in traffic would have been noticed during the mid seventh century, when the Forth was an important part of the so-called 'Columban corridor' which allowed monks and clerics to travel between Iona and their daughter house at Lindisfarne. The island of Inchkeith was reputed to have housed a monastery at this time, under the control of Adomnán, Columba's biographer. This traffic included saints and the relics of saints, along with evangelists, and it was probably around this time that the full-scale conversion of the southern Picts of Fife took place.

The death and burial of one of these holy men, named Ethernan (from the Latin meaning 'eternal'), on the Isle of May led to this becoming an important place of worship and pilgrimage for a period of many centuries. It is probably this individual who was recorded in a contemporary Iona chronicle as dying among the Picts in 669. Recent excavations on the Isle of May have revealed large numbers of early Christian burials under a massive cairn and in two separate long-cist cemeteries, dated to the fifth to tenth century. The oldest building of any substance to survive was a small church of dry-stone construction, which was probably a reliquary chapel built in the ninth century to house Ethernan's shrine(**40**). A further two phases of church building took place on the same site, before David I, in the 1140s, endowed the foundation of a house of Benedictine monks, who were undoubtedly attracted to a site with a pre-existing church, imbued with a heritage of sanctity provided by the relics of this important local saint.

One remarkable discovery, made within the Benedictine church, established an important connection between this local pilgrimage place and the great international shrine of Santiago de Compostela in north-west Spain, thousands of kilometres distant. The burial of a young man, who had died at some time during the fourteenth century, was found in a prestigious location in front of the high altar of the priory church. What was so remarkable was that he had been buried with half a scallop shell placed in his mouth, which had been wedged open (**41**). The scallop was widely used and recognized as the badge of the Santiago pilgrim, and burials have been found throughout Europe with scallops which had been attached to clothing (**90**). Nowhere else however, had a Santiago pilgrim been prepared for his presentation to St Peter in such a fashion. To warrant burial in this location, the young man would have been either an important member of the convent, or an important benefactor, who had made the arduous journey from Fife to Compostela, or had died before completing an intended pilgrimage.

By this time Ethernan's name had been changed to Adrian, and his shrine continued to

41 The author with the Santiago pilgrim's burial, during the excavations on the Isle of May, Fife. The scallop shell can be seen in the wedged-open mouth.

attract more pilgrims even following the destruction of much of the monastery during the Wars of Independence. The island occupied a prestigious location at the mouth of the great waterway of the Forth, and it had a good harbour which was used by vessels carrying pilgrims *en route* to St Andrews, some of whom would have chosen to include St Adrian's shrine as part of their devotional journey. By the time of James IV in the early sixteenth century, the Isle of May was reputed to be one of the chief places of pilgrimage in Scotland, and the island was certainly popular with James for both religious and recreational purposes (see page 106). One tradition has it that barren women who wished to fall pregnant would come here to drink the water of the holy wells and to pray to the saint. The holy well at Pilgrims' Haven survives to this day.

Inchcolm, in the western part of the Forth, has long enjoyed a reputation as a holy island associated with St Columba, dating back to the time when the Forth islands made ideal stepping stones on the holy route from Iona to Lindisfarne. As on the Isle of May, a reformed monastery was established here in the twelfth century, which contained at least one secondary relic of St Columba, a famous image of the saint. The island was within the diocese of Dunkeld, whose Bishops regarded Inchcolm as a shrine of their patron saint. During the thirteenth century, some of the Bishops regarded Inchcolm to be of such importance as to choose it as their place of burial, rather than their own cathedral. The vigil and feast of St Columba was an especially important time of celebration at the abbey of Inchcolm, and in 1256 it is recorded that the Bishop paid for 20 candles to illuminate the high altar during this festival. Conflict with the English during the fourteenth and fifteenth centuries brought troubled times to the island, which was uninhabitable for long periods due to the risk of attack. Praises were sung by the monks to invoke the protection of St Columba, translated as: 'Save this choir that is praising you from attack by the English'.

The first recorded raid was in 1335, when English sailors stole the portable wealth of the abbey, including the image of St Columba. The story has it that when the raiders departed they were soon engulfed by a violent storm, which only abated once they had prayed to the saint for mercy. They landed their booty at Kinghorn and made arrangements for it to be sent back to the island. Walter Bower, author of the famous *Scotichronicon* history, was Abbot during the 1420s, and did much to promote Inchcolm as a cult centre of Columban devotion – the 'Iona of the east'.

The experience of the later medieval pilgrim to St Andrews

Arriving from west or south, pilgrims were drawn to their goal, proclaimed by a multiplicity of boundary crosses, with the tall spires and towers of the cathedral and other churches in the distance (colour plate 4). The sheer scale of the cathedral would have been, as it was intended to be, hugely impressive, especially when first seen with its back to the grey North Sea. This was the largest building in medieval Scotland, and stood within the front rank of great European churches. The Bishops may even have been aware that their cathedral was 12 m (40 ft) longer than its twin apostolic reliquary church at Compostela, whose pilgrimage income they would have dearly loved to match. Pilgrims entered the City of St Andrew by one of the west gates which closed off the ends of the principal streets; those coming from the south would have passed by the beggars at the gates of the leper hospital of St Nicholas, before skirting the outside of the monastic precinct, and coming along what is now Abbey Street. Some found accommodation at St Leonard's, while others were offered a bed in the priory Guest Hall, newly built in the mid thirteenth century on the south side of what is now Pends Road. Visiting monks and clerics might also have been put up here, although some religious institutions maintained their own town houses, such as the great Augustinian abbey of Scone which owned a large residence on North Street.

1 An image of St Ninian (?) with a nimbus, on the base of a twelfth-century copper-gilt crozier head, found in the grave of a bishop at Whithorn.

2 Scott's View: in the middle of the picture is St Aidan's and St Cuthbert's monastery of Old Melrose on a bend in the Tweed.

3 The later medieval monastic precinct at St Andrews, with the Cathedral,
St Rule's, and the ruins of St Mary's Church in line from west to east.

4 The first view of St Andrews for pilgrims arriving from the south, having crossed the Forth on the Earl's Ferry. Scaffolding can be seen to the left where the new Holy Trinity parish church is being built. Early fifteenth century. (Drawn by David Simon).

5 The processional avenues of North Street and South Street converging on St Andrews Cathedral. The remains of the relic chapel can be seen in the east end of the church in the right foreground.

6 Miniature of St Margaret from Robert Blacader's
prayer-book, c 1490.

7 The translation of St Margaret's relics in 1250.

8 Pilgrims at St Margaret's shrine, Dunfermline, on a feast day when the cover of the shrine was removed to reveal the *chasse* beneath.

9 Iona Abbey, with the shrine of St Columba between the west range and the west door of the church, and the island of Mull behind. The Street of the Dead leads to the high crosses, past Tòrr an Aba on the extreme left.

10 The Monymusk Reliquary or *Breac Beannach* of St Columba. Pictish metalwork of the early eighth century. Reproduced smaller than full size, which is 112 mm (4.5in) in length.

11 St Fillan's crozier is formed of two outer cases which date back to the eleventh century, and which originally enshrined the pastoral staff of the saint, who is possibly depicted above the crystal on the drop.

12 James IV being presented to Christ and to St Andrew by St James the Greater, patron saint of the Stewarts. St James is dressed as a pilgrim to his own shrine, with a scallop shell on the brim of his hat. From the *Book of Hours* of James IV and Mary Tudor, 1503.

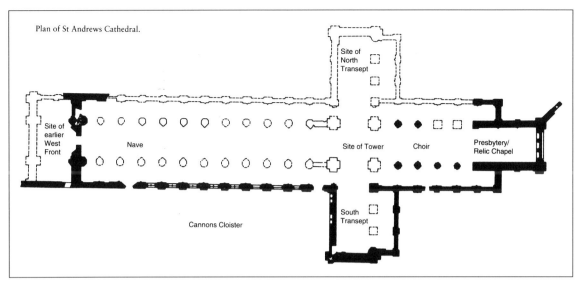

Plan of St Andrews Cathedral.

Site of North Transept

Site of earlier West Front

Nave

Site of Tower

Choir

Presbytery/ Relic Chapel

Cannons Cloister

South Transept

42 Plan of St Andrews Cathedral.

Bishop Robert had commenced the large-scale replanning of the town in the 1140s, moving the centre further west and thus creating a magnificent setting for the successive reliquary churches, as the focus of two main converging avenues – North Street and South Street (**colour plate 5**). Many pilgrims would have arrived in time for the major annual festivals, to mingle with the crowds and to witness the processing of the relics through the streets. Indeed, it has been suggested that the town plan was created specifically to allow a circular processional route without disrupting the market area. The trade guilds of the town, and latterly the scholars from the university (founded 1412), would have participated in the processions, with pride of place being reserved for the canons following behind the relic casket held high under a canopy, escorted by holy statues. In 1290 the Pope granted special indulgences for worshipping in the cathedral at the Feast of the Assumption, at the feast of the Dedication in July, and on St Andrew's Day on 30 November. There was also a feast day of the Coming of the Relics on 6 February. From the early fifteenth century onwards, when the cathedral needed to raise enormous sums for the repair of the fabric, a plenary indulgence, the most important of all, was granted to those attending on the feast of St Michael. This gave remission of all sins, and thereby direct entry into heaven.

On these occasions, pilgrims may have followed the relics in and out of the great west door of the cathedral and through a corresponding gate in the precinct wall; everyday access for the laity would have been by the north porch door in the nave (**42**). Important visitors would have gained access to the precinct through the north side of the Pends gatehouse, dating to around 1350, the stately remains of which can still be seen. This structure, with four lofty rib-vaulted bays, was larger and more impressive than the parish church of the ordinary pilgrim (**43**). Having entered the cathedral, the pilgrims would have been all the while in awe of the sheer scale and beauty of the nave. The pilgrims' stations would have included various altars, as well as taking water from the holy well at the east end of the nave, which was an important pre-existing feature purposefully included in the planning of the church lay-out in the twelfth century. Wells also existed at Dunfermline, Whithorn, and in the under-church at Glasgow, and seem to be an important common feature of these pilgrimage churches. The north and south aisles enabled a continuous flow of one-way traffic beyond the crossing, and towards the relic chapel behind the high altar. Access here was a great privilege

43 Pends gatehouse at St Andrews, from a photograph taken around 1900.

granted only on feast days and other special occasions, although lay folk would have had regular access to the nave, where there were many chantry altars, with priests performing daily masses for the souls of the departed.

The stark ruins of the relic chapel and treasury perceived by the modern visitor belie the riches of what was the most important shrine in the country. Contemporary descriptions survive from the time of Prior James Haldenstone, who played a major part in rebuilding the church following the disastrous fire of 1378, and the collapse of the south transept gable in 1409. Haldenstone needed to raise considerable sums for the restoration, and one of the means used was to issue a circular letter 'advertizing' the relics. He magnified the setting of the shrine especially by the provision of new windows in the east gable which directed more light onto the riches of the shrine (44). Wall cupboards were created for the safe storage of the relics and other treasures, including the crystal cross which had been present at Bannockburn. This space, and that around the high altar, was embellished with painted and gilded statues and other decoration, embroidered wall hangings, as well as tomb effigies (45). The floor level was raised around this time to further emphasize the importance of the shrine, and in the process this enabled the construction of sub-floor tombs,

44 A cut-away reconstruction drawing of the high altar and relic chapel at the east end of St Andrews Cathedral, in the fifteenth century.

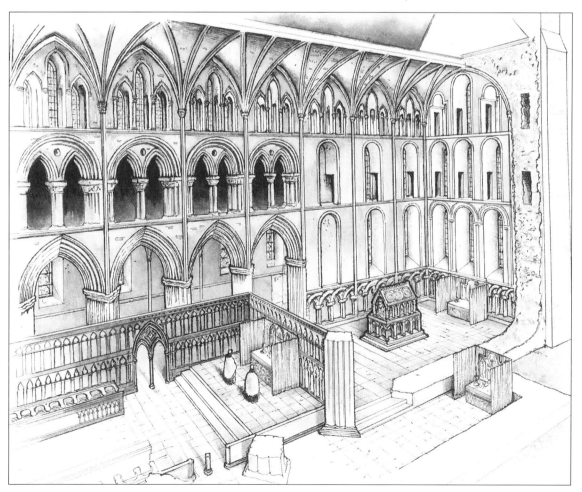

45 Oak statue of St Andrew carrying his cross, c 1500, probably from a screen. The presbytery and relic chapel would have contained a number of statues, similar to this.

including that of Archbishop Alexander Stewart. The overall effect would have assaulted all of the senses of the pilgrims, many of whom would have been making a once-in-a-lifetime visit to this magnificent shrine. Having completed their devotions and given the necessary offerings, the pilgrims were granted a certificate as proof of their piety.

The end of the road?

We have no way of knowing the volume of pilgrims who visited St Andrews, or when the numbers ebbed and flowed. It is likely, however, that this shrine above all others would have benefited from the politically inspired devotional patriotism, which Church and State were keen to promote in the fifteenth century by encouraging a

renewal of interest in native saints and cults. Similarly, we cannot be certain of the international status of the shrine, although it did have some standing, as witnessed in a pilgrimage certificate granted at St Andrews in 1333 to a William Bondolf of Dunkirk, who was sentenced to attend the shrine in expiation of his crime of manslaughter. Interest may have waned by the early sixteenth century; indeed, this is suggested in the foundation charter which converted St Leonard's Hospital into a college of the university in 1512 (**46**). It states that the miracles which attracted constant streams of pilgrims had ceased,

46 Reconstruction of the precinct of St Andrew's in the early sixteenth century. Pilgrims arriving from the south would skirt the walled enclosure along Prior's Wynd in the foreground. The church of St Leonard's hospice and college can also be seen in the foreground. Access to the Cathedral Church was through the precinct wall at the west end, just to the left of the Pends gatehouse in this drawing.(Drawn by Alan Sorrell.)

47 Engraving of the nave of Dunfermline Abbey.

as had the pilgrimages, and that this was due to the fact that '... the Christian Faith, firmly rooted in the land, no longer needed such support'.

On 14 June 1559, the cathedral was sacked by a mob inspired by the Protestant Lords of Congregation and the relics were destroyed. This was not the conclusion of the Scots' secular relationship with the patron saint, nor for that matter was it a final end to religious devotion to his relics. Modern pilgrims can view a relic in St James' Church, St Andrews, and two other relics can be seen in St Mary's, the cathedral church of the Roman Catholic Archdiocese of St Andrews and Edinburgh, at the top of Leith Walk in Edinburgh.

Queen Margaret's shrine at Dunfermline

Margaret was a member of the Saxon royal house, displaced by the Conquest (**colour plate 6**). She sought refuge in Scotland, and in 1070 married the King, Malcolm Canmore (1057–93). Her piety and humility were renowned; she is credited with engineering reforms within the Scottish Church, bringing it into line with current European trends, including the introduction of the first body of monks from one of the reformed orders. The Benedictines established a daughter house of Christ Church, Canterbury, at the royal palace church in Dunfermline, where Margaret was buried after her death in 1093. Some of her own pilgrimages are recorded; she often sought out and rewarded hermits, and a near-contemporary account exists of a failed pilgrimage she attempted to St Laurence's shrine in the Mearns. She was struck-down by heavenly powers when she went to enter the churchyard, and this provides another example of gender exclusion at certain shrines (see page 112). The saintliness of her life was recorded shortly after her death by Turgot, who had been her confessor, and it was this record which laid the foundations for her eventual canonization.

Her sixth son, David I, set about building a remarkably beautiful monastic church and royal sepulchre, inspired by the fabric of Durham Cathedral which was not far off completion in 1128, the year when work at Dunfermline commenced. He levelled and enshrined Margaret's church and the associated royal tombs. The new church was partially completed to allow a consecration in 1150, when David may have overseen the elevation of his mother's remains into a stone monument directly above the original grave (**47**). This location was at the east end of the new nave, which served as the parish church, in front of the rood screen. So at this time the ordinary folk of Dunfermline had easy access to Margaret's tomb, already referred

to as a shrine and accredited with miracles. A monk of Durham, present in Dunfermline in the late twelfth century, witnessed crowds of pilgrims present on what was to become officially recognized as her feast day, and King William the Lion (1165–1214) is thought to have asserted her sainthood long before her formal canonization, having experienced a vision while praying at her tomb in 1199. A list of the miracles performed at Margaret's tomb in the twelfth to thirteenth century has recently been discovered in Madrid.

Early in the thirteenth century, the east end of the monastery church was entirely remodelled, having been completed only 50 years or so earlier (**48**). These major, disruptive works were prompted by the need to create a relic chapel with an associated ambulatory route, and to generally enlarge and embellish the area around the high altar. This was moved a bay further to

48 Sketch of the enlargement of the east end of Dunfermline Abbey, which commenced in the early thirteenth century, doing away with the apsidal end of the church built by David I. The feretory chapel is the block on the left.

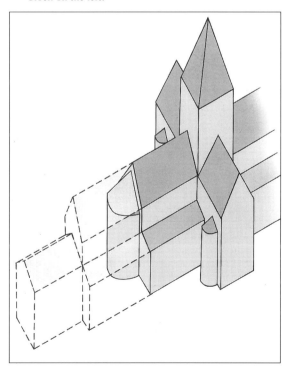

the east, in front of a new, projecting feretory chapel. In 1245, Pope Innocent IV instructed that a report be compiled on the reputed saintliness of the Queen. She was canonized in October 1249, and part of the Pope's Oration read as follows: '...let pious pilgrims on their sacred journey to the shrine of Christ's first chosen Apostle Saint Andrew, find sanctuary and comfort at your shrine in Dunfermline'. This indicates that a visit to Margaret's shrine was a popular detour for pilgrims who had crossed the Forth *en route* to St Andrews. And so the final translation of her relics took place with great ceremony on 19 June 1250, on the day of the consecration of the new choir and feretory (**colour plate 7**). King Alexander III (1249–86) presided, along with Bishop David de Bernham of St Andrews, and Abbot Robert of Dunfermline, who was also the King's chancellor. Her stone monument was opened, and the assembled party witnessed the sweet smell when her remains were exposed (caused by the original embalming of her corpse, but believed to be the odour of sanctity). The bishops and abbots carefully placed her bones in

a new gilded and bejewelled *chasse*, which was carried in solemn procession firstly to the high altar. A major problem was encountered, so the story goes, when they tried to carry her relics past the nearby tomb of her royal husband. Her *chasse* could not be moved another inch until it was decided to translate not only Margaret's remains, but also those of Malcolm Canmore. The *chasse* was eventually placed on a pedestal in her relic chapel. The pedestal was made from polished Frosterly marble, quarried in County Durham and widely used in tombs and altars. It is remarkable that the pedestal survived the iconoclasts and can still be seen today (**49**).

The *chasse* would have been raised up on columns above the marble pedestal; this arrangement is possibly depicted on a thirteenth-century seal of the abbey, where columns are shown supporting a church-shaped superstructure (**52**). This may be an attempt by the seal-maker to represent the shrine, as in the similar example of a seal from Glasgow (see page 21). As well as supporting the superstructure, the columns also created enclosed openings through which the devotees could reach to touch the tomb cover, or to place objects to absorb the radiating sanctity, or to gather up sacred dust. On holy festivals the gilded cover, which normally protected and obscured the superstructure, was lifted on pulleys

49 The marble pedestal for St Margaret's shrine within the feretory at Dunfermline Abbey. Remains of a stone bench and *piscina* basins can be seen.

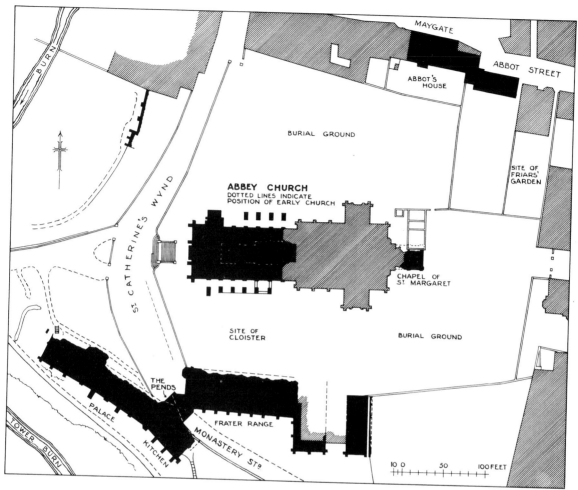

50 Plan of Dunfermline Abbey, showing the outline of the earlier churches under the nave, and the St Margaret's feretory chapel at the east end.

to reveal the beautiful shrine, the top of which was high enough to be seen above the high altar.

The medieval pilgrims entered through the north door of the nave, and followed a path along the north aisle, through the rood screen, and into the north aisle of the choir (50). Even before they entered the feretory, they were heading directly for an altar dedicated to her at the east end of the aisle. It is possible that the head shrine of St Margaret was either displayed here on festival days, or else on the high altar. Here the pilgrims also saw the tombs of numerous Scots royalty, including King David I, who was regarded as a saint by many, and King Robert I, the great patriotic hero. The head shrine comprised a gilded head-shaped case, which could be opened to reveal the partially preserved head of the saint. It is believed that pilgrims could

view locks of her auburn hair set in a crystal on the breast of the head shrine (51). This reliquary was last seen in 1785 at the Scots College at Douai in northern France. The pilgrims then entered the vaulted relic chapel; this still has part of a stone bench which ran around the walls, provided for the comfort of the sick and infirm. The remains of three *piscina* basins can be seen set in the stone bench, each one possibly marking a side altar. These show that pilgrims received the eucharist here. The fact that, unusually, the basins discharged on the inside of this wall, may indicate that the waste from the washing of the sacramental vessels was collected by the pilgrims.

51 Recreation of the lost head-shrine reliquary of
St Margaret, by Walter Awlson, now displayed in the
Abbot House, Dunfermline.

52 Thirteenth-century Chapter Seal of Dunfermline Abbey,
which possibly depicts the design of St Margaret's shrine.

Other relics were displayed in wall cupboards
in the chapel, including the saint's shirt which
was worn by a number of Scots queens during
childbirth, and her gospel book, which had been
miraculously recovered when Margaret herself
had lost it. At these busy times the pilgrims
would have been marshalled out by a southern
route, allowing them to pass another relic altar
dedicated to St Margaret, located in the south
aisle of the nave. Canonization gave Margaret's
cult some degree of international fame, and it is
interesting to note the prominence given to both
Dunfermline and the Queen's Ferry in the map
made by the Englishman Matthew Paris around
1250. The saint's ancestry would have helped to
make her attractive to the English, and this was
certainly the case during her feast day of 16
November 1355, when English soldiers besieging
Lochleven Castle interrupted hostilities to attend
the festivities in Dunfermline. An indulgence of
40 days off purgatory was granted to all who
attended her church on that day (**colour plate 8**).

5
Columba of Iona, and the shrines of Perthshire

That man is little to be envied, ... whose piety would not grow warmer among the ruins of Iona.

Dr Samuel Johnson, October 1773

Columba arrived in the Irish colony of Dál Riata, centred on modern-day Argyll, from Northern Ireland in 563 as a pilgrim serving Christ, having entered into what was considered to be the hardest martyrdom of all, the 'white martyrdom' of exile from his own land and kindred. He was a high-born holy man of the northern Uí Néill royal kin-group, who had become embroiled in warfare and controversy, which had probably compromised his future at home. So, with 12 followers he took ship across the busy North Channel, to a land under the well-established control of neighbours who at least shared the same language and culture as Columba. He was welcomed by Conall mac Comgaill, High King of Dál Riata, who gifted him the small island of Iona off the western tip of Mull (**53**).

The abrasion of time, though tempered by the best efforts of a century of archaeological endeavour, has left almost no clues as to the physical appearance of Columba's monastery. But thankfully this vacuum can be partly filled by the record given to us in the *Vita Columbae* written at the end of the seventh century, possibly to commemorate the first centenary of the saint's death (9 June 597) by his successor

and kinsman, Adomnán, the ninth Abbot of Iona. Adomnán produced a remarkable work of hagiography, recording the often miraculous events of Columba's life, including his efforts at conversion in Pictland, and the establishment of colonizing daughter houses. Most important of all, because Adomnán was writing about events which were almost within living memory, we are given insights of Columba as a real, historical figure, which is not the case with any of the other early saints.

Early pilgrims to Iona

The monastic rule of St Columba required the monks to live a withdrawn, austere, contemplative existence, and so they would not have welcomed constant interruption by large numbers of pilgrims. And yet the fame of the saint, along with the stories of Iona as a sacred landscape regularly visited by angels, would have spread very quickly, back to Ireland, throughout Dál Riata, and with the missionaries taking the gospels across the 'spine of Britain', the mountains which separated them from the Pictish kingdoms to the east and north. Surely this fame would have encouraged pilgrimage to Iona, which was regarded by many as a kind of Eden where heaven spilled over into the profane world. Adomnán does provide some clues regarding early pilgrimage, along with some idea of the physical appearance of the monastery and the island as seen by the pilgrims. He sometimes gives the impression that this was a busy place,

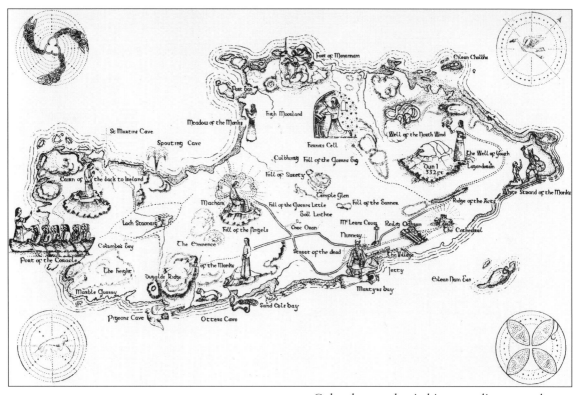

53 Pilgrimage stations on Iona.

and that the provision of hospitality was an essential part of the everyday life of the monastery, with the guest-house being one of the most important buildings. There are hints in the *Life* that visits were possibly of a fixed duration of three days and three nights, during which time the faithful presumably followed a set pattern of pilgrimage devotions at various places on the island. In Adomnán's time, however, access may have been strictly reserved to the high clergy and kings. At other times it is clear that the monks had to be left undisturbed, sometimes with supernatural assistance, for example the storm which blew up immediately after the death of the saint, which ensured that Columba's faithful brethren were left alone to grieve during their three days of doleful funeral rites. Indeed, miraculous control of the elements is a common strand running through Columba's miracles, which is understandable in a country where every aspect of life, especially travel and crop production, was at the mercy of the weather.

Columba was buried in an ordinary outdoor grave, marked by a simple stone, possibly where his 'shrine' now stands to the north-west of the west end of the Abbey church (**colour plate 9**). In Adomnán's time the body still rested there, and no cult of the corporeal relics of the saint had been created. Secondary relics, however, were of great importance; the white tunic worn by Columba when he died, along with books written by the saint, are recorded by Adomnán as having been processed around the fields one springtime to avert a drought at the time of sowing. The fields were in the sandy machair land on the west side of the island, some 2 km (1.2 miles) south-west of the monastery. During this ceremony Columba's books were read from the Hill of the Angels, so named as a place where Columba was seen during his life in discourse with heavenly beings. This is usually identified with Cnoc an t-Sithein, which overlooks the machair from the east side. This may have been one of the places marked by a standing timber cross, mentioned by Adomnán, which do not survive today.

The modern visitor can still see the *vallum*, the earthwork bank and ditch which enclosed the monastic core. This was an important feature for the early pilgrims, as the *vallum* clearly marked the point of entry into the most sacred space (for a detailed description of the early monastery see Anna Ritchie's book entitled *Iona*, in this series). In Adomnán's day the monastery probably comprised a number of buildings with timber walls and thatched roofs, at the heart of which was a group of small churches (54). Nearby were Columba's sleeping hut and his writing hut, which were still in existence at this time, and no doubt treated as sacred structures. The latter is associated with the rocky outcrop, known as Tòrr an Aba, just to the west of the rebuilt church, where excavations have revealed the base of a structure about 3 m (9.9 ft) in length that may have faced east to the churches. The evidence of Adomnán's writings may well overlap with the archaeological evidence in the possible identification of his *magna domus* (great house), which functioned as a place of assembly, teaching and recreation. A large circular timber building was found at the southern limit of the enclosure, just north of the burial ground at Reilig Odhráin, with a diameter of about 18 m (59.4 ft), the construction of which has been dated to at least a generation after the death of the saint. If not the great house, perhaps this could have been the guest-house, divided up into sleeping cubicles for the pilgrims, and purposefully sited near to the entrance to the monastery.

Pilgrimage stations on Iona

One of the recent excavators at Iona, Jerry O'Sullivan, has described the entire landscape as a 'consecrated place, resplendent with Divine favour'. It is possible to suggest, for the early Christian period at least, that we should not simply consider the pilgrimage in the context of a single focus at a shrine, but rather in terms of a focus and many satellites, the latter being outlying chapels and burial-grounds, along with

54 An imaginative reconstruction of Columba's monastery on Iona.

other places associated with events in the life of Columba. This is the concept of *an toras*, the journey, still alive in the Irish pilgrimage tradition at places such as Glencolmcille in Donegal, north-west Ireland, involving a circuit around a number of related sites. On Iona, O'Sullivan considers these places and markers as 'mnemonic devices ... physical clues which guide and structure ritual action'. The pilgrims would have known instinctively how to react at these spots: what to do, what prayer to say, although this is lost to us now. They may also have been helped and guided in their responses by the monks, or by inscriptions such as the one which existed at the base of St Martin's Cross, which could only have been read by worshippers on their knees, facing east to one of the original churches. This high cross, and the others now dedicated to St Odhráin, St John and St Matthew, are indicators of the support of wealthy patrons in the eighth and ninth centuries, and would have served as the clearest possible markers for pilgrims (55).

Early pilgrimage may have featured a circuit which culminated at the shrine, by which time the pilgrim would have been in a heightened

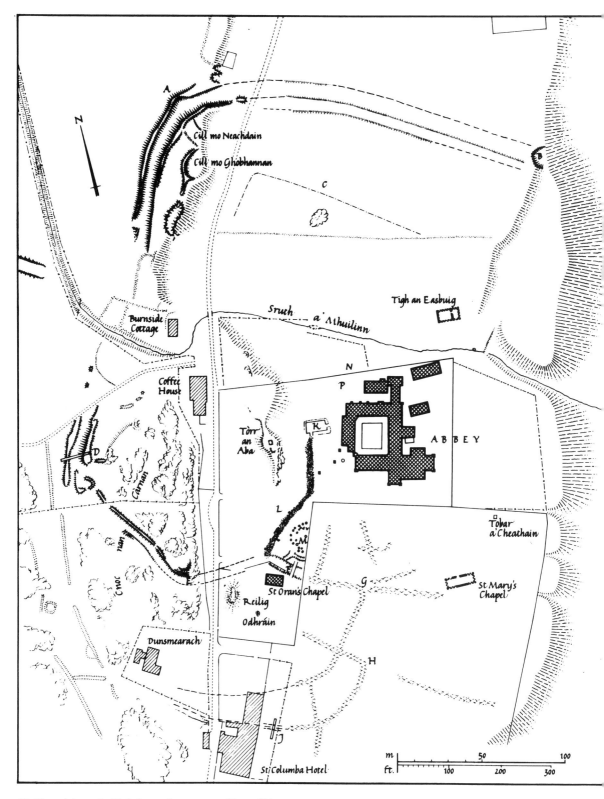

55 Plan of the early Christian enclosure around Iona Abbey.

emotional and spiritual state. Many of the pilgrims would have travelled in the same kind of *curragh*, a skin boat with oars and sails, as the one in which Columba and his companions arrived at Iona. Most would have landed at the Bay of the Martyrs', so-called after the slaughter of a large body of monks here by the Vikings in 806, just to the south of the modern pier, and facing Mull across the Sound of Iona. Others may have sought to further replicate Columba's experience by landing at St Columba's Bay, at the south end of the island, where cairns of beach pebbles can be seen, probably created by pilgrims. The creation of such cairns can still be seen as a living tradition with tremendous longevity, for instance at Colmcille's Well, which is one of the stations on the Glencolmcille pilgrimage, where each pilgrim carries up three stones while saying prescribed prayers. It is important to remember that pilgrims travelled to Iona in death as well as in life. The chroniclers tell us of Irish Kings who ended their days on Iona in 'pilgrimage and penitence', and this tradition of Iona as the most prestigious sepulchre, emphasizing the great sanctity of the place, was continued by the Kings of Scots until this role was transferred to Dunfermline in the late eleventh century. There were at least nine medieval cemeteries on Iona, all of which may have featured as pilgrimage stations. The burial-grounds with chapels would certainly have figured in this postulated circuit, including the chapel at the hermitage burial-ground, Cladh an Dìsirt, 500 m (550 yds) north-east of the monastery.

This important funerary role is reflected in the name of the main street, Sraid nam Marbh, the Street of the Dead, which is still followed today from the harbour to the Reilig Odhráin burial-ground, and on to the monastery. This cobbled road was the grand processional route used by funerals and by pilgrims, marked by a trail of ornamental crosses, chapels and burial-grounds, with side paths leading off directing pilgrims towards some of the satellite sites. The street led pilgrims to the royal burial ground, entering the holy precinct by an entrance through the *vallum*

which would have been marked by a high cross. The ultimate focus, marking journey's end for the pilgrims, was the great cross of St John standing sentinel in front of St Columba's shrine; this cross has the widest span (2.2 m/6.6 ft) of any high cross in Britain or Ireland. This is vast in comparison to the tiny, understated shrine chapel, probably built in the tenth to twelfth century, which is believed to enclose Columba's original grave, although excavations have shown that any evidence of this function has been destroyed by later burial activity. This would have been a free-standing building which formed part of a group of early churches, originally constructed in timber. Traces of stone walls of pre-thirteenth-century churches were uncovered when the nave floors of the abbey church were lifted early this century. This concentration of devotional structures, including the high crosses, the churches, and the shrine, helps us to visualize how the site would have looked through the eyes of pilgrims from the eighth century until the arrival of the Benedictines in the thirteenth century. An approximation of this can only be replicated now by visiting sites in Ireland such as Clonmacnoise or Glendalough, although the same combination of features would also have been experienced by early pilgrims at St Andrews, Whithorn and possibly Glasgow.

History of the relics

As well as possessing miraculous powers, Columba's relics became increasingly important as symbols of spiritual and secular legitimacy, in reinforcing the authority of abbots, bishops and kings. The corporeal relics may not have been elevated from the saint's grave and enshrined until around the middle of the eighth century. It has been suggested by the architectural historian Ian Fisher that three of the early high crosses on Iona, along with the creation of the *Book of Kells* in the Iona scriptorium, were events related to the celebration of the enshrinement at this time. The bones may have been translated to rest within a simple corner-post shrine, a composite stone box, no more than 1m (3.3 ft)

56 Reconstruction of a corner-post shrine. (Drawn by Alan Braby.)

in length, fragments of three of which have been found in rubble at the abbey and at Reilig Odhráin. Such a box would probably have been placed in the largest timber church at the monastery, and would have contained secondary relics such as Columba's tunic, with the bones themselves in one or more decorated caskets inside the box (**56**). The multiplicity of shrine fragments can be simply explained in the context of there being a number of saints, or possibly kings, enshrined at Iona; Adomnán himself became a saint after his death in 704.

In the seventh and eighth centuries the Abbots of Iona were at the head of a federation of monasteries following the rule of St Columba in Scotland and Ireland. The Abbots travelled between these monasteries, taking with them a group of secondary relics, representing the physical manifestation of their authority. This group included Columba's bell, pastoral staff, gospel book and tunic, as a well as a portable shrine reliquary. The relics were only moved for important reasons, such as to be in attendance at the promulgation of laws, or the consecration of churches, or when the relics were in danger, as was increasingly the case at Iona where Viking raids are recorded in 795, 802, 806, and 825. In response to this, in the early ninth century, a major new monastery was constructed at Kells in Co. Meath, which marked the beginning of the dispersal of St Columba's relics from Iona. It was this dispersal which may eventually have brought a relic of Columba to Glencolmcille sometime in

the ninth century. It is interesting to ponder on whether the nature of the pilgrimage circuit still current at Glencolmcille is at all indicative of the nature of pilgrimage on Iona at the time of the dispersal of the relics. The Viking raid of 825 is especially famous due to the martyrdom of a monk named Blathmac who was slaughtered while successfully protecting the relics from discovery. An account made soon after informs us that this portable shrine was made of 'precious metals wherein lie the holy bones of St Columba'.

The relics played an important part in Kenneth son of Alpin's take-over of Pictland in 842–3. As part of this political process, Kenneth built a new church to honour the relics at the existing Columban monastery at Dunkeld in Perthshire, which has been described as the gateway between the Highlands and the Lowlands. The church at Dunkeld was located on a key strategic site beside an ancient fortress guarding an important crossing of the Tay. The continuing danger of Viking raids on the exposed coastal monastery at Iona contributed to a major division of the relics between Kells and Dunkeld which took place around 849. Relics dispersed to Dunkeld, probably including the main shrine, were moved again, this time to Kells, due to the threat of Viking attacks on eastern Scotland in 878. Iona was not abandoned however, and pilgrimage continued. After all, the tradition of the reverence of the sacred places on the island inhabited by Columba was older and more ingrained than was the veneration of his relics.

Life on the island continued to hold danger, with the last recorded Viking massacre of monks taking place at the end of the tenth century. Irish monastic life was still being practised in the later eleventh century when Margaret, saint and queen, provided offerings to help repair the fabric of the monastery. Her actions are not unusual, especially when viewed in the context of Iona as the burial-place of her royal father-in-law, Duncan, and is also helpful in illustrating the continuing devotion to the cult even from the distant east-coast power-base of the kingdom.

Cradle of the north wind

An unusual artefact which is traditionally associated with pilgrimage can be seen outside the west door of the Abbey. This is a massive granite block with a shallow basin in the top, and decorated with an equal-armed cross at one end (57). One tradition is that the stone had to be scrubbed (creating the shallow basin) by a virgin to obtain a favourable wind for travel. An alternative interpretation is that this was used as a foot bath for pilgrims, who would always have participated in ritual cleansing before entering the church.

Benedictine Iona

In the later twelfth century, amongst great controversy, the sub-kings of the Isles shifted their patronage away from the traditional Irish monastic practices of the old Iona monks, in favour of a community of Benedictines, who were established on the island by Reginald, Lord of the Isles, in around 1200. This prompted an extraordinarily intensive period of ecclesiastical construction, which had already commenced in the middle of the twelfth century with the building of new burial chapels at Reilig Odhráin and at Cladh an Dìsirt. As construction at the abbey commenced, a new church, dedicated to St Michael, was rapidly built just to the north to provide an interim place of worship for the Benedictines. This later became the infirmary chapel. At the same time, a convent was being built for a body of Augustinian nuns 400 m (455 yds) south of the abbey, located close to the old church of St Ronan's which was rebuilt as a new parish church for the growing lay population of the island, initially made up of builders and craftsmen employed on these building projects during the first decades of the thirteenth-century. St Mary's Chapel, 60 m (200ft) south-east of the abbey, was also built at this time, and is believed to have served as a pilgrims' chapel (58). The care and comfort of pilgrims may have been shared between the monks and the nuns of the two religious orders.

This revitalization of the ecclesiastical complex must have coincided with a revitalization of the cult, and indeed many aspects of the construction campaigns can be related to the re-creation of the infrastructure of pilgrimage. The Benedictines were either consciously repackaging the Columban pilgrimage experience, or were simply reinvesting in a long-established pilgrimage

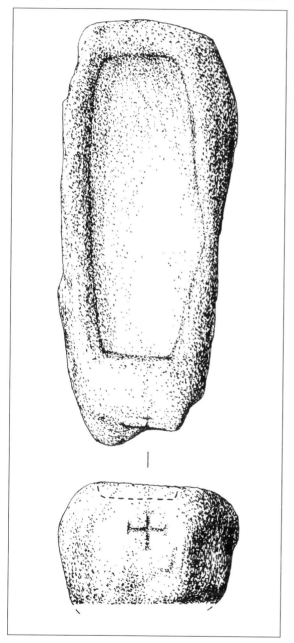

57 The 'cradle of the north wind' – a possible pilgrims' foot bath from Iona Abbey.

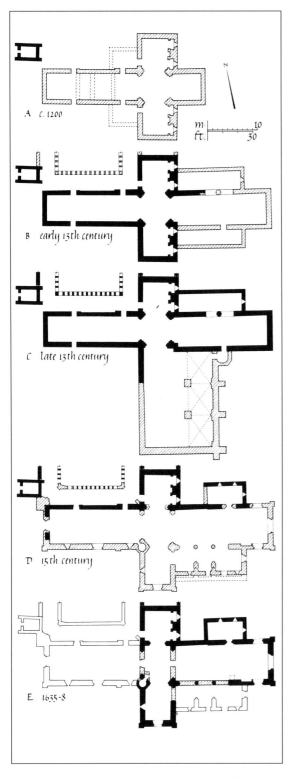

A c. 1200

m | 10
ft. | 30

B early 13th century

C late 13th century

D 15th century

E 1635–8

58 Plans showing the development of the Iona Abbey
    church.

apparatus, in which the whole island was 'an
arena for controlled access and ritual'. The paved
Street of the Dead was resurfaced and enlarged to
a width of 2.4 m (8 ft), and geophysical surveying
of the area to the south of the abbey has revealed
a complex pattern of paths and ditches, all of
which would have been part of a system designed
to control pilgrimage traffic. This included a path
allowing access from the main route off to St
Mary's Chapel. Columba's possible writing cell
on Tòrr an Aba was further emphasized around
this time by the erection of a cross, the base
foundation of which was found in excavations. A
cobbled plaza was created around the west end of
the abbey church, in front of Columba's Shrine,
St John's Cross, and the well-head. The latter
may have had a liturgical role since early
Christian times, and would have been an
important feature of later pilgrimage as a source
of holy water to return home with.

The Iona cult in the late medieval period

The only relic on Iona to be recorded in the later
medieval period is the 'hand of St Columba',
which may well have been enshrined within the
earliest phase of the church of the Benedictines.
It is believed that the original cult focus was
located in the north transept, where two
recessed altar stances can be seen, flanking a
central niche which once contained a statue,
presumably of the saint (59). This transept may
have been set aside for the reception of pilgrims,
until the cloisters were built onto the north side
of the church. The east end of the church was
largely remodelled early in the thirteenth
century; this extension encompassed a steep
slope to the east thereby requiring the
construction of an undercroft, introducing new
liturgical possibilities into the physical
arrangement of the cult. At the upper level the
choir extension would have enabled a shrine
chapel to be provided behind the high altar, all
of which was raised up on a timber floor, the
scarcement for which is still visible. The 'crypt'
was partly excavated by MacGregor Chalmers
around 1910, when it was found to have only

2.5 m (8 ft) of headroom, but occupied the full width of the east end (5.2 m/17 ft), with an internal length of 11.5 m (38 ft). Part of the undercroft space can still be viewed through a floor grille located adjacent to the south choir arcade (**60**). The plain, unvaulted ceiling in the

59 Niche for a statue, probably of St Columba, in the north transept of Iona Abbey.

60 Sketch plans of the two-storey remodelled, thirteenth century east end of Iona Abbey. (Drawn by Peter MacGregor Chalmers, who excavated the undercroft in around 1910.)

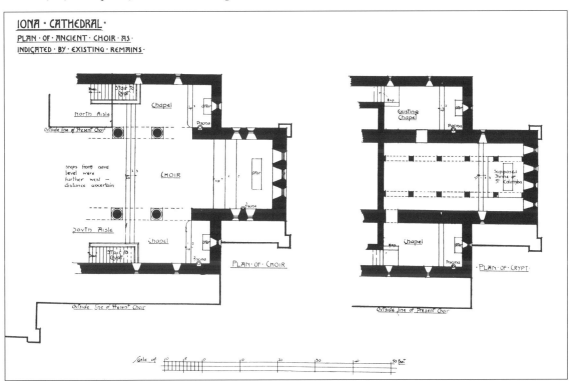

undercroft was probably supported by two or more central timber posts, with some natural light provided by windows. The eastern extension included large aisles to the north and south of the choir, and these enabled a one-way ambulatory system for pilgrims, with a two-storey arrangement of shrine altars.

Pilgrims would pass by the high altar to carry out their devotions at the upper shrine, before entering one of the flanking aisles, both of which contained steps in the west part down into the undercroft and the lower shrine. This arrangement is well illustrated in the north wall of the choir, viewed from the south, where the early thirteenth-century choir arcade stands high-and-dry above the original floor scarcement, and above the much altered remains of what was a doorway within the undercroft (**61**). This reconstruction is supported by the fact that crypts were very much in fashion at this time, notably at the other major cult centres of Glasgow and Whithorn, providing a heightened dramatic setting for the cult along with multiple opportunities for veneration.

In the late thirteenth century a further remodelling, this time of the south transept, began, the purpose of which was to create a hugely enlarged space with direct access to and from the undercroft. The newly planned transept was four times as large as the original with three vaulted chapels forming the east part. At the north-east corner was a doorway leading from the transept into a spiral stair tower, which allowed access up to the choir and down to the undercroft. This may have been planned for the purpose of rehousing the main shrine within a space which could accommodate larger numbers of pilgrims, fully articulated with the lower focus of the cult. Work on the new south transept was abandoned in the fourteenth century, probably due to the general disruption caused by the Wars of Independence.

The south transept area may have been left unresolved until an ambitious building campaign was led by Abbot Dominic (1421–c 1465). A papal bull of the 1420s refers to the timberwork

61 North wall of the choir at Iona, showing the scarcement (bottom left) for the thirteenth-century choir floor-level and arcade, with a remodelled doorway which was originally within the 'crypt'.

of the choir collapsing, presumably into the crypt, which may well have prompted the rebuilding. In 1428, the Abbot petitioned the Pope to grant an indulgence of three years off purgatory to all pilgrims visiting Iona on Columba's feast day. This might have boosted pilgrimage and thereby provided extra income to help pay for the building work. The undercroft was infilled and the choir floor-level lowered. It is possible that the former had already ceased to play an important part in the pilgrims' experience at the abbey, although veneration of a shrine here was still very much alive. This is illustrated by the gift at this time of a new gold and silver reliquary for the hand of St Columba by Donald, Lord of the Isles (died 1421). By this time most of the Iona pilgrims would have been Gaels from Ireland and from the west highlands and islands. The shrine would have attracted only those eastern and lowland Scots with a special devotion to the saint; after all, they had much easier access to the two major eastern Columban shrines at Dunkeld and Inchcolm. This should not detract from our appreciation of Columba as a revered, national saint, referred to in a late medieval invocation as *spes Scotorum* – 'the hope of the Scots'.

The tomb of Alexander Macleod on Harris

A remarkable sixteenth-century panoply of saints is preserved in the church of St Clement's at Rodel, Harris, in the Outer Hebrides. The church was built by Alexander Macleod (died 1546), chief of the Macleods of Harris and Dunvegan, who broke with the funerary tradition of his ancestors, and rather than being buried on Iona, had a richly decorated, recessed wall-tomb built

for himself (**62**). The arch framing the tomb features a slightly confused Litany in stone of the 12 Apostles, along with carvings of the Holy Trinity and the Virgin and Child. All of these were being invoked to protect the soul of the deceased.

St Columba and Dunkeld

In transferring relics of St Columba to an impressive setting in the church at Dunkeld in 849, as recorded in the *Scottish Chronicle*, Kenneth son of Alpin was demonstrating the powerful protection he and his dynasty received from a saint who was already familiar to the Picts now living under Scottish rule. The relics also underpinned the status of Dunkeld as the chief church of the new kingdom. Nothing of the early churches can be seen at Dunkeld, although this period is represented by a small group of sculpted stones of ninth- to tenth-century date. One of

62 Tomb of Alexander Macleod in St Clement's Church in Rodel, Harris.

these, the so-called Apostles Stone, features on a side panel a large figure of a hooded cleric, which may be the oldest representation of Columba to survive (**63**). Amongst the relics was St Columba's crozier, now lost, which was named *Cathbhuaidh*, meaning 'yellow battler', or 'battle victory', due to its use as a battle standard. The earliest record of this is when the crozier helped the Scots army defeat the Vikings at the Battle of Corbridge in 918. Saints' pastoral staffs were important relics and symbols of inherited ecclesiastical power. These became considerably altered and embellished by the addition of decorative cases, to the extent that almost nothing survives of the original simple wooden objects. Evidence exists to show that Columba's crozier was still venerated in the later medieval cathedral at Dunkeld, built on the site of the earlier churches. The obverse of the Chapter Seal, dated to the early thirteenth century, provides an extraordinarily clear depiction of the arrangement of reliquaries as experienced by the medieval pilgrims (**64**). The crozier is shown above or behind a high-quality, church-shaped *chasse*, all of which was presumably displayed behind the high altar. The gifted craftsman who

63 St Columba (?) on the Apostles Stone, Dunkeld Cathedral.

64 Thirteenth-century Chapter Seal of Dunkeld Cathedral, showing the crozier and shrine of St Columba.

65 The Kilmichael Glassary bell-shrine, 148 mm (6 in) in height, with attached cross and chains.

made the seal matrix has included on each side an angel wafting incense over the sacred objects.

The Chapter Seal may also provide a clue as to the identification of an important reliquary which has hitherto remained anonymous. The seal shows a chain and cross hanging from the end, or drop, of the crozier. The Kilmichael Glassary bell-shrine was found in Argyll along with such a chain and cross which had been added in the twelfth century, and which were probably used to suspend the bell-shrine from its side loops (65). Cormac Bourke of the Ulster Museum has now made the fascinating suggestion that these objects may actually be represented together on the seal, this arrangement being entirely appropriate because '...the bell and staff were the twin insignia of rank of the early ecclesiastics'. Were this to be true, then the Kilmichael bell-shrine can be identified, possibly along with the Monymusk Reliquary, as the only Columban relics to

survive in Scotland. This having been said, there is a chance that the Guthrie bell-shrine, another of the National Museums of Scotland's treasures, may also have had an Iona connection, having once been in the possession of the Lords of the Isles (66). Bell-shrines are known in Scotland and in Ireland, the earliest comprising a decorated case of silver and bronze which enshrined a small iron bell of early Christian date, believed to have belonged to a saint. The Kilmichael Glassary shrine had a hole cut in the bottom of the case, possibly to allow contact with the bell inside. These small bells had started life as functional objects used to regulate worship and assembly during the monastic day.

The choir and feretory of Dunkeld were rebuilt during the thirteenth to fourteenth century; rebuilding of the nave then followed in the early fifteenth century. At some time during this period the high altar was provided with a beautiful ante-mural of painted and gilded panels depicting the 24 miracles of St Columba. Mentioned in medieval documents, this is one of the numerous treasures destroyed during the Reformation. The importance of Dunkeld as a reliquary church is further reinforced by surviving records which reveal that a fragment of the True Cross had been obtained by the canons of the cathedral. The evidence of the major building works, coupled with evidence of rich reliquaries and other decoration, suggests the existence of vigorous pilgrimage devotional activity, which would have attracted additional offerings to the cathedral. The medieval pilgrim would have seen the church at the centre of a complex of other important buildings, including a fortified bishop's palace, with houses for the canons nearby. Pilgrims would have been accommodated in the hospital of St George, which was located at the centre of the burgh.

Columba's other secret weapons

The crozier shared a talismanic warlike quality with two of Columba's other relics, the *Cathach* and the *Breac Beannach* (see page 89). The

66 The Guthrie bell-shrine, 210 mm (8.5 in) in height, modelled around an early Christian iron bell. The silver-gilt figure of God the Father and the two bishops were added around 1300.

Cathach, meaning 'battler', is a psalter possibly written by the saint, which may have been taken to Ireland in the ninth-century dispersal, and enshrined in a silver casket in the eleventh century (67). For hundreds of years this was carried into battle by its hereditary keeper ahead of the O'Donnell clan. Saints' books were a common form of secondary relic, although none has survived from Scotland, with the possible exception of the Gospel book of St Margaret (see page 74).

The so-called *Breac Beannach* of St Columba, also known as the Monymusk Reliquary, is one of the most highly prized artefacts in the collections of the National Museums of Scotland (**colour plate 10**). This is the only reliquary associated with the saint to have survived, and even more importantly this was a battle talisman which inspired Scottish armies for hundreds of years, and, as they believed, helped them to secure victory at Bannockburn. What is even more extraordinary is that all this could be represented by a tiny wooden box, decorated with enamel and fitted with bronze and silver plates in the shape of a miniature tomb-shrine. Tomb-shrines made from stone panels survive beside some early churches in Ireland and probably existed in Scotland as well. Three similar reliquaries are known from Ireland, and two others, presumed to be Viking loot, have been found in Norway. The Monymusk Reliquary is only 11 cm (4.5 in) in length by 9 cm (3.5 in) in height. It was made by a Pictish

67 The *Cathach* of St Columba: a psalter possibly written by the saint, and enshrined in a silver casket in the eleventh century.

craftsman early in the eighth century, when it was provided with fittings for a neck strap, which has led some to believe that its original function was as a pyx, a kind of portable container used by a priest in which to carry the consecrated host. The Gaelic name probably means 'speckled gabled one', which describes both the shape and the decorative effect of the metalwork. It was large enough to have contained only a small bone or secondary relic of St Columba.

The assumption has long been made that this is the *Breac Beannach*, although there is no absolute proof of this identification. As such, this may have come to Dunkeld with the other relics in 849, although the earliest reference to the reliquary is when it was granted to the monks of Arbroath by William the Lion before 1211. At this time it was probably kept in the abbey church, which also had a relic of St Thomas Becket, to whom the abbey was dedicated. The invocation of St Thomas in King Robert's address before the battle (see below), might suggest that the abbot also brought the reliquary of the martyr from Arbroath to the battlefield. The abbot was responsible for attending the army with the *Breac Beannach* along with an armed escort. This was a great honour, but dangerous nevertheless, and Abbot Bernard was quick to relinquish this duty after Bannockburn in 1314. He granted the reliquary and its lands to Malcolm of Monymusk as hereditary keeper, where it was probably kept from then on, until its discovery there in the nineteenth century. Both armies came to Bannockburn with relics, as was common practice at the time, each side believing the power of their saints to be stronger than those of the opposing army. The *Breac Beannach* is likely to have been held within a larger decorated box so that the soldiers would have

been able to see what was providing them with heavenly protection. We also hear of at least two other relics which would have been paraded to inspire the Scots. The Crystal Cross may have been taken there from St Andrews Cathedral, along with the relic of St Fillan which so inspired King Robert I. More than 100 years later, Bower quotes the King's address to his men before the battle which illuminates the importance of the invocation of heavenly support, rallying the saints to their just cause:

'This day is a day of rejoicing: the birthday of John the Baptist. With Our Lord Jesus Christ as commander, St Andrew and the martyr St Thomas shall fight today with the saints of Scotland for the honour of their country and their nation.'

St Fillan of Glendochart

Our understanding of the cult of St Fillan is based around the personal devotion of King Robert I to the saint, coupled with the surviving, paired relics of crozier and bell (**68 and colour plate 11**). This cult developed in a very different way to most of the others, with an important emphasis being placed on the symbolic legal power of a group of seven relics. In this case it would seem that pilgrimage centred around a reliquary church was only of secondary importance. St Fillan may have been an important pre-Columban missionary who established one or more churches which persisted within the route which ran from Tyndrum to Loch Tay. Fillan's cult persisted in this area, known as Glendochart, throughout the Columban period and beyond, having an important influence on one of the main routes from Dál Riata into what had been the Pictish heartland of Atholl and Strathearn. The cult was revitalized by King Robert I (1306–29); Bruce spent time as a fugitive in Glendochart in 1306, where he believed himself to be under the protection of St Fillan.

The arm of St Fillan may have been among the reliquaries taken to Bannockburn (**69**). Legend has it that this was the luminous left arm, the light from which helped the saint to

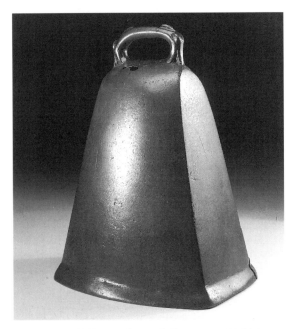

68 St Fillan's bell: a cast bronze bell, 290 mm (11.5 in) in height, made in Scotland in the twelfth century. This was kept in the churchyard at Strathfillan, where it was used to cure diseases until the end of the eighteenth century.

write. On the eve of the battle, so the story goes, the King was praying to God and to St Fillan, although he was unaware that the Abbot of Inchaffray had purposefully left the bones behind for safekeeping. During his prayers, the reliquary was heard to click open and then shut. Upon inspection it was then revealed that the bones had miraculously returned to their case, which was no doubt taken to be a good omen. Fillan's support of the cause against England would have made him even more popular with the Scots. In 1318 King Robert I endowed an Augustinian priory to be created, as a daughter house of Inchaffray, on the site of the ancient monastery on the River Fillan near Tyndrum, creating an establishment which would better serve pilgrims.

The relics were each kept by individual hereditary keepers, or dewars (Gaelic *dèoraidhean*), and only gathered together into the church on feast days, especially on 9 January. Each relic was associated with lands in the glen which provided for the dewar and the relic. Apart from the surviving bell (*bearnán*) and crozier (*coìgreach)*, there was also the arm shrine, manuscript or altar, shrine or mallet, chalice, and healing stones. The relics represented the law within Glendochart, which remained a busy routeway throughout the medieval period and appears to have been lawless as a result. Rather than simply being symbols of ecclesiastical power, the relics carried with them special jurisdictional powers, and were used especially in the recovery of stolen cattle and other stolen property. This was a chief drove-road for cattle being moved from the west highlands to market in central Scotland.

The crozier comprises an outer silver gilt case of fourteenth-century date, which encloses an eleventh-century bronze crozier head; nothing of the original wooden staff survives. The terminal

69 Hand-shrine of St Patrick: the lost, later medieval Scottish hand- and arm-shrines of St Giles, St Fillan, St Ninian and St Columba, would probably have resembled this fourteenth- to fifteenth-century Irish reliquary.

70 A graveslab found at St Fillan's Priory, decorated with a cross and what may be a representation of the arm-shrine.

of the outer case features a possible image of the saint along with a large crystal which was credited with healing powers. Indeed, all of the relics were used as part of a healing cult for sick people and animals. The cast bronze hand-bell, which is twelfth-century in date, was used in connection with the healing of lunatics, which involved dipping them in the Holy Pool on the river 1 km (1090 yds) north-west of the priory, and then taking them to the church and placing the bell on their head. This and other pilgrimage rituals continued into the nineteenth century. James IV paid for the dewar of the bell to attend his coronation at Scone in 1488, and subsequently visited Glendochart a number of times on pilgrimage.

A remarkable recent discovery has strengthened the evidence of devotion to the arm shrine. A graveslab, carved with a roughly executed image of an arm attached to an encircled cross, was found by Niall Robertson at the priory (70). This may well have marked the grave of one of the keepers of that reliquary.

6
St Magnus and the Orkney shrines

The martyrdom of Earl Magnus in 1116 led to the creation of a major pilgrimage centre within Scandinavian Scotland at Kirkwall in the Orkney Islands. This is the only great pilgrimage church in Scotland to have retained its relics, the presence of which determined the very existence of the church, as well as its design. The other remarkable aspect of this legacy is that we can still experience much of the original setting of the pilgrimage within the beautiful, largely unaltered cathedral, the design and construction of which proclaim its origins in the Romanesque style of the twelfth century. Not only do we have the surviving physical manifestation of the cult as represented by the cathedral, but we also have a reliable narrative explaining the mix of politics and piety from which the cult arose. This is documented in the *Orkneyinga Saga*, written less than 100 years after the events (**71**).

The life and death of Earl Magnus

The Norse Earls ruled Orkney from the late ninth century; the Scandinavian peoples were newly converted to Christianity by about AD 1000, which would still have been regarded as a young and fresh faith in Magnus' lifetime. The people would have been predisposed to embrace the concept of a holy martyr of their own, in addition to which they were already familiar

71 St Magnus' Cathedral, Kirkwall.

with the existing cults of the royal martyrs established in Norway and Denmark.

The sagas provide few clues of Magnus leading an especially saintly life, apart from his un-Viking behaviour while on campaign with the King of Norway during the Battle of the Menai Straits in 1098 (**72**). The *Orkneyinga Saga* tells how he refused to take any part in the fighting but instead read from his psalter and chanted psalms. The King accused him of being a coward and hiding behind his faith. Following this, Magnus embarked on a period of six or seven years of self-imposed exile. He returned to Orkney in the early 1100s to assert his claim to be ruler in tandem with his cousin, Earl Hakon Paulson. This they achieved successfully for about seven years, according to the saga, until their partnership turned into a rivalry. A peace meeting was arranged to take place at Easter 1116 on the island of Egilsay, where the Bishop probably had a residence. This went wrong, and culminated with Earl Hakon's supporters demanding the execution of Magnus, which was carried out by Hakon's cook, who killed Magnus with an axe blow to his head. We are told that the barren place of execution, 400 m (520 yds) south-east of the church on Egilsay, was miraculously transformed into a verdant meadow soon after the murder, as it remains to this day, now marked by a memorial stone.

Burial at Birsay

Magnus' body was carried by sea and by land for burial in the cathedral of Christkirk near the Earl's palace at Birsay. It is unclear as to whether this was on the mainland or on the nearby tidal island known as the Brough of Birsay. It seems likely that by this time the Bishop's church was on the mainland, and excavations under the present parish church in the village of Birsay have revealed part of a twelfth-century precursor of good quality construction. The grave quickly became renowned as a place of miracles and heavenly fragrances, although popular devotion to the cult was officially suppressed by Earl Hakon and by his son, Earl Paul. Hakon did go

72 Fifteenth-century statue of St Magnus from Kirkwall Cathedral.

on pilgrimage to Rome and to the Holy Land, which may have been in penance for his part in the murder. This denial of the cult was also led by Bishop William, even in the face of miraculous cures, and even though he successfully invoked Magnus' intercession to obtain a fair wind on a voyage home from Shetland.

The Bishop was persuaded, however, and this was an integral part of his shift in allegiance to another rival, Earl Rognvald. He was the saint's nephew, who had been garnering support to gain control over Magnus' half of the earldom. Rognvald embarked on this course of action, according to the saga, having first entered into a bargain with the saint, promising to build a magnificent new church for the relics, in return for heavenly protection and support. In this passage of the saga, the saint is addressed 'as though alive and effective still'. Bishop William executed the first part of this process, about 20 years after the martyrdom, by elevating the bones of the saint from his grave into a shrine which was placed above the altar in Christkirk. Rognvald decided to build a cathedral to house Magnus' relics, and so in 1137 the shrine was carried in solemn procession over the 25 km (17 miles) between Birsay and Kirkwall. Rognvald was aware of the strong, traditional support for Magnus which existed in this part of the island, which he translated into support for his cause, so closely identified with the interests of the saint. There was already a good harbour and small trading port at Kirkwall, and Rognvald realized the potential to create a centre for his earldom here, with the movement of the relics symbolizing the shift in power from Birsay to Kirkwall.

The shrine was first installed in the existing church of St Olaf, while the arrangements for founding the new cathedral were made. We know that the portable shrine was decorated with precious metals, because of an account of the theft of gold and silver from this while it was kept in St Olaf's. Building work commenced immediately in 1137, and after only five years enough of the east end was complete to allow the translation of the relics and the dedication to take

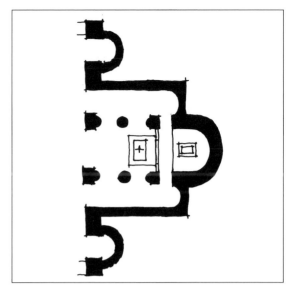

73 Sketch plan of the original twelfth-century east end of Kirkwall Cathedral, with St Magnus' shrine in the apsidal feretory chapel.

place on 13 December 1142 (**73**). Rognvald was murdered in 1158, having fulfilled his vow to his saintly uncle, and was buried in his cathedral. He was subsequently canonized in 1192.

And so the trio of holy places associated with St Magnus was complete – martyrdom at Egilsay, burial at Birsay, and enshrinement at Kirkwall. These three stages are also apparent, albeit within a single church, in relation to the martyrdom of St Thomas at Canterbury. This parallel, and the more obvious one of the *martyria* of Christ – crucifixion, entombment, and ascension – would not have been lost on the cathedral clergy at Kirkwall, who would have been at pains to relay this comparison to the faithful.

The Mass Roads and the Mansie Stones

The longevity and strength of devotion of the Orkney people to their patron saint is expressed in their veneration of the route and stopping places on the route taken in moving the body and the relics of the saint between the holy places. The routes taken between Egilsay, Birsay and Kirkwall are commemorated in the landscape with the persisting Old Norse place-name *Messugate*, translated as Mass Roads. One of these converges on the village of Birsay, and not the Brough, strengthening the belief that the grave was at the former. Parts of these routes can be followed today on the evidence of place-names, and by following stones, known as Mansie (Magnus) Stones, which reputedly mark where the body, or relics were rested. Few of these stones survive today, but it is possible to retrace Magnus' posthumous travels.

The most direct route from Egilsay to Birsay would have been by boat around the coast. However, this would have involved passing through the treacherous waters around Eynhallow, and so instead the body was taken by boat across the short passage to Evie and then by land on to Birsay. There is reputed to be a Mansie Stone at a place once known as Mansie's Grip at the north end of Loch Swannay, with another on the burial mound at Crustan, with a distance of 2.6 km (1.7 miles) between the two. An elderly farmer showed this author one Mansie Stone, now much reduced in size, which is well hidden at Northside of Birsay (grid reference HY 258 287). The route taken by the relics in around 1136 from

74 Plan of St Magnus' Cathedral showing the thirteenth-century enlargement of the east end. The relics were rediscovered in the two piers immediately to the west of the original apse.

Birsay to Kirkwall can also be reconstructed. The first stop, in Birsay parish, is well documented and visible. The Manse (Magnus) Well is on the road east from the village near Boardhouse Mill; this is where the bones were reputed to have been washed, and consequently the spring is always pure, and never runs dry. In recent times, a pump superstructure was added, now redundant, but a mug has been thoughtfully provided for the use of passers-by (HY 257 274). A Mansie Stone stands a few metres away on the other side of the road.

Pilgrimage to the shrine of St Magnus

The shrine attracted devotees from the Norse peoples of Caithness, Orkney and Shetland, as well as from further afield. The relics were also dispersed as far as Iceland to satisfy the demands of more distant devotion. The Romanesque cathedral at Kirkwall was built by masons trained at Durham and Dunfermline; the plan grew from the need to allow access to the shrine which was originally located in a semicircular apse behind the high altar, similar to Cuthbert's shrine at Durham. An ambulatory was created which allowed pilgrims to move between the aisles of the choir and around the shrine in the apse, via a passage behind the high altar (**74**). Here they were screened from view, thus avoiding any disruption to the canons in the choir

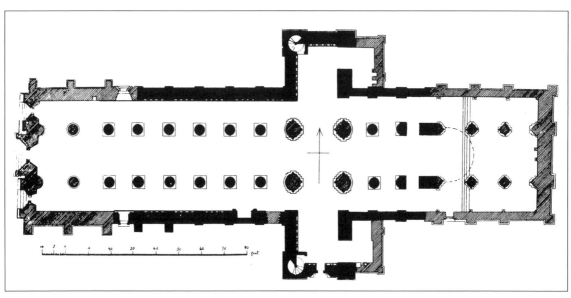

75 Crucifix pilgrims' badge mould from St Magnus' Cathedral.

stalls and the celebrants at the altar. Although well planned, the space for pilgrims was limited, and so the decision was made in the early thirteenth century to demolish the Romanesque east end and to rebuild this with an additional three bays. This allowed more space for a proper feretory chapel, in response to growing numbers of pilgrims, especially at the feast of the martyrdom on 16 April. It is interesting to note that whereas extreme conservatism is displayed elsewhere in the architecture, an architect with flair and imagination was employed to glorify the new feretory. The pilgrims would have returned home with badges bought at the shrine, possibly including the crucifix badge made in the mould found in or near the cathedral (75). The shrine was further glorified by providing first the new east end, and eventually the whole church with high vaulting, putting it on a par with St Andrews and with Nidaros Cathedral at Trondheim, Norway, which was probably the intention of the Bishops and Earls.

The churches at Egilsay and Birsay, along with the Mass Roads, would have featured in the pilgrimages of serious devotees (76). The church at Egilsay where Magnus prayed before his death, was replaced by the existing church which was probably founded around the same time as the cathedral in 1137. The architecture of this church illustrates a different set of economic and cultural links to those of the cathedral. This church, with its round tower, can be paralleled with buildings in north Germany and in East Anglia.

Relics and artefacts

During restoration works at the cathedral in 1848, workmen discovered human skeletal remains hidden within a mural chamber in the third pier from the east end, on the north side of the choir, 2.7 m (9 ft) above the floor. These were heralded to be the relics of St Magnus, although this was proven to be incorrect when a similar discovery was made in the corresponding pier on the south side of the choir in 1919 (77).

76 St Magnus' Church, Egilsay, close to the place where the saint was martyred.

What was so remarkable about this partial skeleton was that the skull exhibited evidence of a fatal axe-wound to the back of the head, matching precisely the saga accounts of the martyrdom of the saint. It seems highly likely that the relics found in the north pier are those of St Rognvald. Magnus' relics were in a small box of Norwegian pinewood, 75 cm (30 in) long by 25 cm (10 in) wide, which is on display in Tankerness House Museum in Kirkwall (78). This plain box would have been the inner container for the relics, which sat within a decorated *chasse*. These mural interments have been interpreted as crude measures to hide the relics, probably carried out at the time of the Reformation. The neatness of the storage arrangements, however, coupled with the symmetry of symbolism, does indicate the contrary. The location is significant, being close to where the shrine stood in the apse of the first

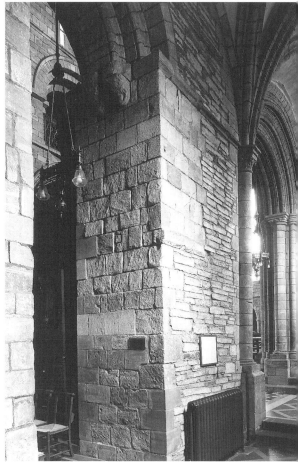

77 The south pier in the choir of St Magnus' Cathedral where the relics of the saint were rediscovered during renovations in 1919.

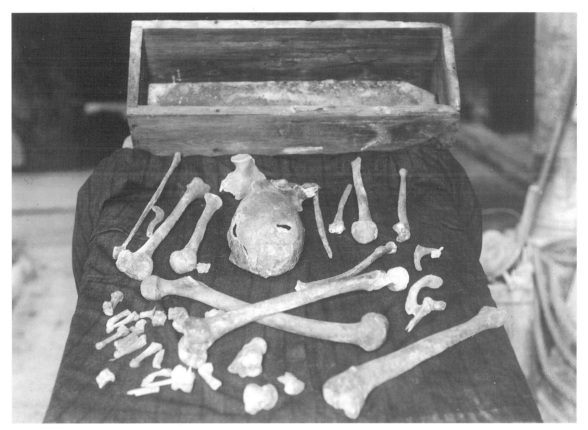

east end, and close to the high altar in the later arrangement. It is possible that the location does reflect the position of either relic cupboards, or a beam above the high altar where reliquaries of these twin founding saints were displayed in more settled times.

78 The relics of St Magnus and the box in which they were found. The skull displays the fatal axe-wound.

Shrines on Papa Westray

This is one of the most northerly of the Orkney islands, located on the safest sea route between Orkney and Shetland, which was probably a significant factor in relation to the development here of Pictish saints' cults. It is possible that this strategic location was exploited by incoming Northumbrian bishops in the early eighth century, who had been invited to convert the Picts of the Northern Isles to Roman Christianity, the Pictish King Nechtan having shifted his allegiance away from the Celtic Church. The discovery of a fragment of a Pictish corner-post shrine of eighth-century date at St Boniface's Church on the west side of the island

has highlighted the importance of this site as a place of pilgrimage from early times. Excavations have shown that this had been an important place of settlement for around 1000 years before the church arrived.

Enduring traditions of pilgrimage at St Boniface's and at St Tredwell's on the east side of the island both seem to have grown from the purposeful adoption of ancient, and possibly sacred, pre-Christian sites at the time of conversion. Tredwell can be equated with St Triduana of Restalrig (see page 51), and both are likely to be manifestations of the rehabilitation, by incoming Christians, of a native Iron Age water-sprite goddess' cult. St Tredwell's originated as an island broch or crannog, which became built-up over a long period of time, until it was no longer isolated (**79**). Until recently the track leading to the site

79 The ruined pilgrimage chapel of St Tredwell, Papa
    Westray.

was called Messigate (Mass Road). Chapels
were built here, the last probably dating to the
fourteenth century. Popular pilgrimage for
healing purposes persisted at St Tredwell's into
the nineteenth century, against the wishes of the
Protestant Church. This involved the devotees
completing a number of circuits of the site,
barefoot or on their knees, bathing in the loch
waters, and leaving an offering of a coin.
Excavations in 1879 recovered 30 coins of post-
medieval date from the floor of the chapel.
These forms of rituals were also reported at the
Brough of Deerness, a high coastal promontory
site on the east coast of the Orkney mainland,
with origins in the eleventh century.

7
James IV: Scotland's pilgrim king

James IV (1488–1513), a worldly European prince, was also a devoted pilgrim, who took time out from the politics of Church and State, from the affairs of chivalry and diplomacy, and from battles with rebellious nobles, to venerate the relics of his favoured saints. In doing so, he was probably both reflecting and encouraging the last *floruit* of popular pilgrimage in Scotland.

His devotional and penitential actions seem to have been driven by personal guilt for his own participation in the rebellion which resulted in his father's death. He became known as 'James of the Iron Belt' because of the heavy chain he is reputed to have worn next to his skin, as a constant reminder of his sins, to which he added another link each year. He did manage however, to mix piety with pleasure while on pilgrimage, and we know this thanks to the Lord Treasurer's accounts which record where the King spent money and for what purpose. The accounts provide a real insight into the circumstances of his pilgrimages. Indeed, this forms the most detailed information concerning the peregrinations of any individual Scot in the medieval period, albeit a far from typical, royal personage.

His first pilgrimages started soon after his accession following the murder of his father in 1488. He was only 20 when he made his first recorded journey to St Ninian's shrine at Whithorn in 1491, and from 1493 St Duthac's at Tain in Easter Ross was added to the annual itinerary. The southern pilgrimage usually took place in spring or summer, the northern one usually in the autumn (**80**). It is interesting to note that these visits never coincided with the saint's main feast day, although it is possible that some of the visits were arranged around lesser festivals. An alternative explanation is simply that the King attended at times which suited him, and that the very nature of his presence made each visit a special occasion. He was occasionally in Whithorn for Easter, although sometimes he would spend this sacred time on retreat, for instance at the Greyfriars monastery in Stirling.

James' year of pilgrimage

Between March and September 1507, at the age of 36, James chose to spend about six weeks on pigrimages; twice to Whithorn, along with visits to Tain and to the shrine on the Isle of May, covering a total distance of more than 13600 km (850 miles). This was an intense example of the King's personal devotion to these shrines in particular, which was a constant aspect of his religious life.

The intensity of James' pilgrimage activity in 1507 was primarily motivated by his concerns for the health of his wife, Margaret Tudor, and for their new-born, and his first legitimate, son, James. And so on 10 March, believing that his own sins would lead to a terrible judgement on his Queen and heir, he took affirmative action to redeem himself in the eyes of God, by setting out on foot with a small entourage on an arduous pilgrimage to the shrine of St Ninian at Whithorn. Travelling south-east from Edinburgh

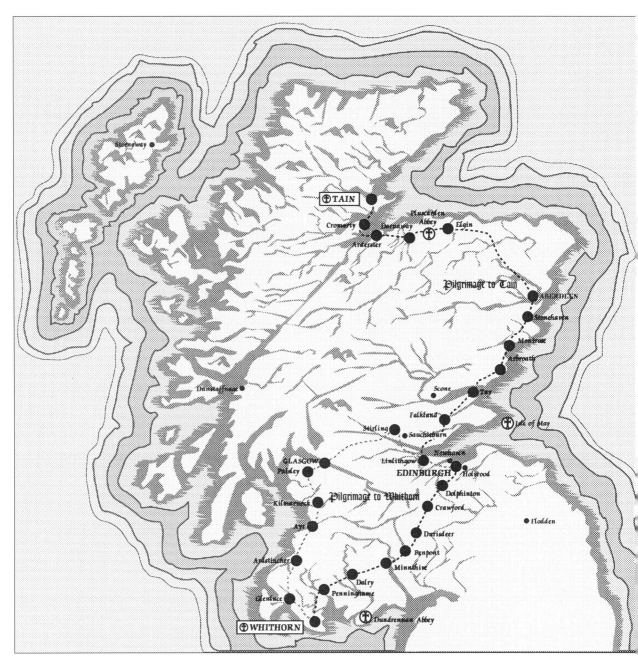

80 Map showing the pilgrimage routes of James IV to Whithorn and Tain.

by Crawford, stopping after five days at Penpont to have his shoes resoled, he managed to complete the whole journey in eight days, averaging 32 km (20 miles) per day. On reaching Wigtown, rather than rest for the night in comfort, he engaged a guide to lead him through the darkness by the shortest paths, so that he could arrive at the shrine in time for morning mass, footsore and penitent.

He believed that his prayers were answered as his wife and son recovered thanks to 'the piety and devotions of her husband, through the help of St Ninian under God'. The Queen was well enough to accompany her husband on another pilgrimage to Whithorn in July 1507 to offer her own thanks to the saint. This journey there took about two weeks, travelling on horseback as was normal, going via Glasgow, Paisley and Kilwinning, where offerings could have been made to relics in each of the great churches at these places. At night the royal party would have been given hospitality by important churchmen and nobles, and some nights were spent as the guests of monasteries – Crossraguel, Glenluce, Wigtown and Tongland were all conveniently located for this purpose, as was the priory at Whithorn itself (**81**).

The King's year of pilgrimage continued at the end of August 1507 with a voyage from Edinburgh to venerate the shrine of St Adrian (Etheran) on the Isle of May in the Firth of Forth, and spending some time in Crail, Fife, where he was entertained by the priest. The Treasurer's accounts helpfully list the disbursements of monies, showing that the King and his party needed two boats, and that another was hired to take 'the kungis dynar and the cuke' to the island. On 26 August the King gave an offering of 14 shillings to the hermit who tended the shrine. This is a sum which is often repeated in the accounts as being given in offering at various shrines and altars, and was presumably a recognized and acceptable amount.

Only two days after returning to Stirling Castle from his trip to Fife, James set off once more, this time to the shrine of St Duthac at Tain in Easter Ross, which, along with Whithorn, was his most favoured holy place, where he went on pilgrimage at least 18 times. Like his march to Whithorn earlier in the year, this trip to Tain was also exceptional in that he chose to ride alone, and completed the journey in only two days. He rode furiously from Stirling to Aberdeen and then on to Elgin, covering a remarkable distance of 208 km (130 miles), where he slept, fully clothed for a few hours on a priest's dining table, before setting off again and completing the last 64 km (40 miles), including the two ferry crossings at Ardersier and Cromarty, to arrive in time for morning mass.

Piety, politics and pleasure

This last trip especially has been used to characterize James IV as both pious and impetuous, as well as vigorous and strong, but not surprisingly the matter is more complex. The two-day ride to Tain was rather better planned than it might seem, in that the King had been provided with a purse of £26, and that household members had been despatched in advance, possibly to check that the route was safe, and to have fresh horses and food ready. The story of this trip would have gained immediate currency, and would certainly have served to impress his subjects with his vigour, as well as stressing how successful the King had been in enforcing the rule of law throughout his kingdom, making it possible for him to undertake such a journey in safety, carrying a large purse. Or else he may simply have been attempting to set a record, possibly as a wager.

From a political viewpoint, his two favoured places of pilgrimage could not have been better located. Both were in outlying parts of the kingdom which had traditionally been hostile to royal control. Tain had formed part of the Earldom of Ross, which had been forfeited by the MacDonald Lords of the Isles in 1475. The Lordship of the Isles was then forfeited in 1493 after James' campaign against the Islesmen, which was also the year of his first pilgrimage to Tain. Unrest in the Isles continued, however, and so in September 1506, James combined a pilgrimage to Tain with a meeting with his master gunner, who had come hot-foot from the successful siege of Stornoway, the last stronghold of MacDonald power. This insightful King knew how to make himself popular, and distracted his northern subjects from their traditional loyalty to the clans by spending time amongst them, sharing their veneration of a beloved local saint.

While on pilgrimage he disbursed largesse, and contributed even more to the local economy by attracting greater numbers of pilgrims, with money to spend on necessities and offerings. His annual, and sometimes even more frequent,

81 The cloister of Glenluce Abbey, where James IV stayed *en route* to Whithorn.

visits to the shrines at Whithorn and Tain would have become popular events, with many coming to catch a glimpse of their King, and to enjoy the processions, and shows of wealth, as well as benefiting from the greater access to the relics which the presence of the royal household afforded.

By no means did the King and his court travel incognito; such a large and richly dressed group, accompanied by drummers and musicians would have been immediately recognized by his subjects, as was undoubtedly the intention. Almost every trip to Whithorn was by a different route, allowing James to be seen by the maximum number of his subjects, and to make offerings to hermits, and to a great range of churches and chapels *en route*. During the pilgrimage to Tain in October 1505, and to Whithorn in 1508, and probably on other occasions, the party included four Italian minstrels, an exotic sight indeed to the eyes of the ordinary farming folk. Many who met with the King were treated generously; alms were given to the poor and sick, and the accounts are full of payments to inns, ferrymen, pipers, jesters, as well as the cost of feed and ale for the horses. Building works were almost constantly underway at many of the churches and monasteries which featured in his itineraries, and these are illustrated by the regularity with which the King gave 'drink-silver' to the masons.

Some of the days were spent in hunting and hawking, especially during the autumn northern pilgrimage, and the royal hounds and huntsmen were included in the entourage. The evenings were spent in playing cards, sometimes for marathon sessions during which James was known to lose very large sums. Musical entertainment was essential, sometimes provided by portable organs, known as 'regals', which were carried with the baggage. James IV was also renowned for his extra-marital alliances, and pilgrimages regularly involved the company

of his current mistress. His third and most enduring mistress was Janet Kennedy, whose residence of Darnaway Castle was conveniently situated on the road to Tain, between Elgin and Inverness. On at least one occasion (October 1501) she accompanied the King from Fife to St Duthac's, and in April 1503 'Janet bare ars', as she was known, was installed in Bothwell Castle to welcome James *en route* to Whithorn.

Royal pedigree of pilgrimage

James IV was following and enlarging traditions of royal pilgrimage which reached back to the time of Saint Margaret, and probably earlier. We know of no other Scottish King who invested as much time, expense and effort in pilgrimage as he did. Pilgrimage probably featured in his upbringing, and we know that his mother, Margaret of Denmark, possibly accompanied by his father, set off on pilgrimage to Whithorn in 1473 soon after his birth. James III's possible interest in a pilgrimage to the Holy Land is described below (see page 120).

While marching to Whithorn along the Borders tracks in 1507, James IV was himself considering a pilgrimage to the Holy Land. He was already especially favoured by Pope Julius II, who was at that time arranging for a papal emissary to deliver special gifts, including the present Sword of State, symbolic of his favour to James. Such a pilgrimage would raise him further in the eyes of the Church, elevating him as the first Scottish king to visit Jerusalem. James certainly investigated this possibility, and it seems likely that the pilgrimage undertaken by Archbishop Blacader in 1508 was to serve as a reconnaissance trip (see page 120). By 1509 James had lost interest, and instead was considering participating in, or even leading a European crusade. To do so would certainly have staked his place in posterity, after all the great King Robert I had only posthumously sent his heart into battle against the Turk. But the renewed threat from England put an end to James' crusading ambitions.

In addition to his public devotions, James also upheld the private devotion of the Stewart family to St James the Greater of Compostela. The personal bond between James IV and his saintly namesake is well illustrated by the portrait of James attended by the saint in full pilgrim's garb, depicted in his Flemish *Book of Hours*, produced around 1502 as an expensive wedding present (**colour plate 12**). James is known to have sent a silver ship to the shrine of Santiago de Compostela, which might possibly have symbolized his wish to voyage to Spain and to present himself before the shrine of his patron saint. Royal devotion was continued by James V (1513–42) who spent money on reliquaries for the bones of St Duthac and St Adrian (Ethernan) which he kept in his possession.

James on pilgrimage to the Isle of May

The King enjoyed a summer pilgrimage to the shrine of St Adrian on the Isle of May, giving him an opportunity to sail around the Forth in the newly constructed naval vessels of which he was so proud. These trips followed a standard pattern: setting sail from the ports of Leith or Newhaven, James would spend a few days either on board ship or else being given hospitality in the Fife ports of Anstruther or Crail. The royal party might occupy more than one ship, and in 1503 one was used just to convey the choir of the Chapel Royal in Stirling Castle to the Isle of May to sing a mass. In 1506 he was transported on the newly launched 700 ton warship *Margaret*, while in 1508 he used the warship *Lion*. James was carried by these large vessels to the Fife ports, where smaller boats were hired with local crews who were familiar with the harbours on the Isle of May.

The King enjoyed the company of his great retired admiral, Sir Andrew Wood of Largo, on his visits to the Isle of May, and only two weeks before his death granted lands to Sir Andrew in return for which 'the grantee and his heirs should accompany the King and Queen on their pilgrimages to the May, whenever required'. By this time the monastery on the Isle of May was in ruins, and the pilgrimage was focused on a small chapel appended to a hermitage and

pilgrims' hostel in the rebuilt west range of the priory. The shrine was tended by a hermit who enjoyed the King's generous offerings, in return for which he once gave James a seal, and on another occasion he turned up at court in Edinburgh with a gift of plump rabbits which thrived on the island.

James on pilgrimage to Tain

The northern pilgrimage offered a limited choice of routes, compared to the number of variations on the Whithorn route; most trips to Tain were by way of the east coast burghs – Arbroath, Montrose and Aberdeen – then heading north-west to Elgin and Inverness. The more arduous highland route north from Perth was used occasionally. James usually lodged in Inverness or Fortrose the night before arriving at the shrine. While in Tain, he was entertained by the Provost of the town.

The subject of James' veneration, St Duthac, was reputed to have been a native of Tain, and returned there to base his episcopal ministry following a period of study in Ireland. He is often associated with a bishop of the same name who is recorded in the *Annals of Ulster* as having been buried in Armagh in 1065. The fact that his relics included characteristically early accoutrements, however, namely a bell (presumably complete with bell-shrine) and a staff, might suggest that Duthac lived at some time during the eighth to the tenth century. He may have been the Abbot of Iona recorded in an obituary in the *Annals* for the year 937.

By the thirteenth century the saint had attracted considerable popularity. In 1418 a petition for his canonization was compiled by Prior James Haldenstone of St Andrews, and submitted to the Pope. This adopted the standard form of listing his miracles from both before and after death, and emphasizing his current popularity. The widespread nature of the cult is well illustrated by the number of chapels and altars throughout eastern Scotland dedicated to St Duthac, ranging from Orkney to St Andrews, Linlithgow, Edinburgh and

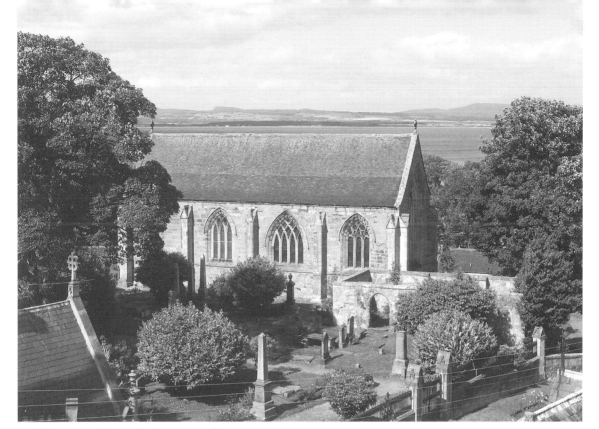

Haddington. Although the main relics were at Tain, others were in royal hands, and in St Machar's Cathedral, Aberdeen. The King took his own relic of Duthac with him on pilgrimage to Tain in October 1503. He maintained his devotion to the saint even when not in Tain, for example by giving offering at the altars of St Duthac in St Giles' Cathedral and Holyrood Abbey in Edinburgh.

The cult at Tain was focused on not one, but three separate churches which housed the relics at different times. All three featured in James' pilgrimage, and can still be seen today. The King would have entered the churchyard enclosure from the south, where he would have been confronted by two churches, the nearest being the small reliquary chapel built in the later twelfth century (**82**). The first connection between Duthac and the royal house was established here in 1321 when William, Earl of Ross endowed six chaplainries in the chapel to say masses for the soul of Alexander III. The place had an infamous earlier royal connection however; the same William had been guilty of violating the legal status of sanctuary held by

82 The fifteenth-century collegiate church of St Duthac at Tain, with the ruins of the twelfth-century church in the foreground.

Tain, when he seized the wife and daughter of King Robert I who were sheltering here in 1306. The small chapel was badly damaged during a local skirmish in the 1420s, by which time it was a growing collegiate foundation. This prompted the construction of a larger church, completed by 1459 with fresh endowments from James II, which effectively served as a royal chantry, that is where priests performed daily rounds of masses for the souls of the king and royal family. Tain, along with other churches, benefited from the current fashion of endowing collegiate foundations, which coincided with a renewed interest in native saints which was being promoted by the Scottish Church. The collegiate body numbered around 12, being a significant number related to the number of Apostles, and included a sacristan who was responsible for the relics and other treasures. The clerics housed in buildings around the churchyard, including a common hall and kitchen, which would have been very familiar to James IV.

James would have entered the church through a large southern porch, now gone, which was probably provided for the benefit of pilgrims, who would have congregated and sheltered here. The porch and the churchyard would have played an important part during the busiest times of pilgrimage, as did the Links Chapel, because of the limited space available in the main church. The interior was divided into two by a rood screen carrying a representation of the crucifixion scene, and fronted by side altars. The King would have passed through a central door in the screen to enter the more sacred space of

the choir, to be confronted by the relics displayed in all their glory, with the most important displayed on a tabernacle on the high altar (83). The relics were normally kept in the wall cupboards, known as aumbries, still visible in the north wall of the choir, and ordinary pilgrims may have had to make do with a brief glimpse of these, having given a coin to the assistant sacristan to encourage him to open the cupboard doors. Other relics were kept in the sacristy, as it is recorded that James made separate offerings to the relics here. The sacristy was located at the south-east corner of the church, but was demolished some time ago. Each reliquary altar had a secure offering box, known as a *stok,* where pilgrims of all ranks placed their donations.

The Links Chapel, by the beach, was built around the middle of the twelfth century on the

83 The east end of St Duthac's, Tain, where James IV venerated the relics of the saint. The wall cupboards can be seen, where the relics were secured.

reputed site of Duthac's birthplace. This was the original reliquary church, but by the time of James IV it was in a dilapidated state, in the care of a hermit who received offerings from the pilgrims.

The relics and reliquaries of St Duthac

The relics at Tain included St Duthac's head in a silver head shrine, his breastbone in a gold reliquary, and other bones in a portable shrine of silver gilt with gold, along with his sark (shirt), cup, bell and pastoral staff. The head shrine was not an ancient object, having been made during the 1480s and gifted by Thomas Monylaw, the first Provost of the college. Duthac's sark was believed by the Earls of Ross to give miraculous protection against injury, although this did not work for Hugh, the fourth Earl, who was killed while wearing it at the Battle of Halidon Hill, near Berwick, in 1333. The shirt was returned to Tain by the English, out of respect for the saint. Around 1500, the saint's cup was taken around Scotland by a pardoner, supposedly raising funds for the fabric of the shrine. A travelling pardoner from Tain is also recorded as being in Stirling in 1508. The staff and bell may have featured in the royal procession at the shrine, headed by the King and the Provost of the college, who was also Provost of the town. The accounts record monies given to the individuals who carried these objects, who may have been hereditary keepers.

As well as giving money offerings, James also enabled the embellishment of the shrine, utilizing the skills of the royal goldsmith. Some of these are recorded: in 1497 he gifted a silver case for a cross, costing over £6; in 1508 he provided a silver reliquary weighing 55 ounces; in 1511 the saint's shirt was repaired by the royal embroiderers; and in the same year another reliquary was made, this time with more careful thought to thrift, from 'ane of the auld silver platis brokin' of the royal dinner service.

At the time of the Reformation in 1560 the main relics, in their precious cases, were given by the Provost into the safekeeping of his kinsman Alexander Ross of Balnagowan. Uniquely, the receipt listing these survives, which is more than can be said for the relics, which were never seen again.

Heaven turned against the King

James IV last pilgrimage to St Duthac's shrine was on 8 August 1513, only a month before his death at the Battle of Flodden, alongside possibly 10,000 other Scots. This was viewed by the English as an almost miraculous outcome, many of whom gave thanks to St Cuthbert, whose protection they had invoked before the battle. It is ironic that the death of Scotland's pilgrim king was attributed to the intercession of another saint, taking his enemies' part.

8
Scots Pilgrimage Abroad

Medieval Scotland has been characterized as a small, outward-looking country, which needed international contacts to enable economic and cultural development. The number of people, however, who travelled to achieve these ends was small compared to the volume of pilgrims. The Scots were drawn to the great shrines in the Holy Land, Rome and Santiago, as well as to shrines in England and on the Continent. Travel to local and national shrines paled into insignificance compared to the great hardships involved in the pilgrimage to the Holy Land, but this remained the ultimate goal of both the devout poor, and those who had the resources to enjoy some comfort along the way. With the exception of some of the latter, the hardships of overseas pilgrimage would have deterred all but the most seriously religious. The great efforts required were equally balanced with the greatness of the spiritual rewards (84).

By the twelfth century, and probably much earlier, we know that Scots were a familiar sight on the Via Francigena, the pilgrimage roads to Rome. Viewed from a Roman perspective, Scotland had always been considered as the uttermost end of the earth, earning special respect for the pilgrimage efforts of the Scots. They had a characteristic garb which helped identify them from other nationalities; we learn this from the writings of an Abbot of Bury St Edmunds, concerning a dangerous journey he undertook in about 1160 to Rome on Church business. This was a time of violent turmoil in northern Italy, caused by a schism between two rival Popes. To avoid detection he disguised himself in the ragged outfit of a Scotsman, walking barefoot with his shoes over his shoulder 'after the fashion of the Scots'. When approached, he shook his staff and used 'threatening language after the manner of the Scots'!

Preparation

Pilgrims would seek royal protection for their property and family until their safe return, as specified in laws dating back to the reign of David I (1124–53), if not earlier. A letter of licence from the Crown was required, and it was illegal to leave Scotland without this document, although it is possible that this was only applied to the nobility. Both clerics and laity could obtain letters of commendation, and safe conducts had to be obtained from the English King if the journey involved travel through his realm. A licence from the Church would enable the pilgrim to receive the sacraments in foreign lands and to solicit alms; one such licence was issued to William Brown, a pilgrim to Rome and Compostela, by Bishop Henry Wardlaw of St Andrews. This also granted an indulgence to those who gave alms to the pilgrim. Service owed to feudal lords was suspended for the duration of the pilgrimage. The wealthy could arrange to have funds deposited at mercantile centres along the way. If the pilgrim died, however, the family would have had considerable difficulty in

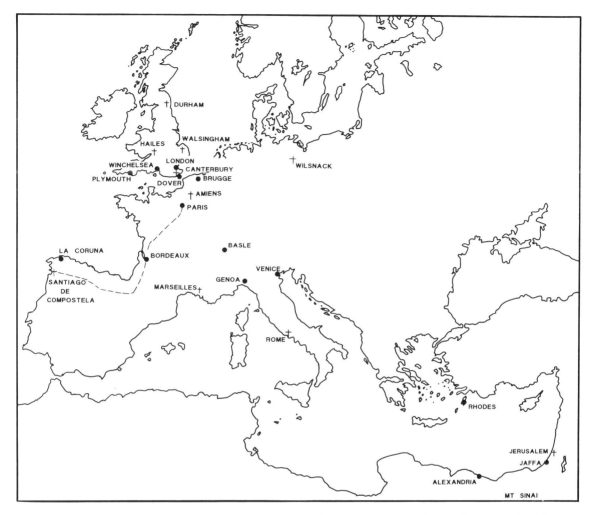

84 Scots pilgrimage abroad: the principal shrines are marked with a cross.

obtaining the return of these funds. The better-off would travel in groups on horseback, whereas the poor pilgrims travelled on foot, relying on hospice accommodation and alms to be provided by the transnational networks of religious houses, and by pious individuals. Guides and itineraries could be consulted for information regarding routes, language, diet, inns, and what to do once at the shrines. One such famous and influential guide, entitled *On the Holy Places*, was written by Abbot Adomnán of Iona, based on the first-hand account told to him by Arcluf, a Gaulish bishop who had been shipwrecked in the Hebrides on returning from a pilgrimage to the Holy Land. Practical guides would have been a common feature of the libraries of monasteries and cathedrals. Glasgow Cathedral was no exception, and owned one guide which combined a list of Lenten Station Churches in Rome, with a list of other Roman churches and shrines where indulgences could be obtained. Many pilgrimages were inspired by word-of-mouth reports, spread by returning pilgrims, or else by representatives of shrines travelling around to publicize their holy place. In 1520 an emissary from the famed monastery of St Catherine on Mount Sinai was in Edinburgh to raise cash for this shrine by enrolling members in a confraternity.

Immediately before departure, pilgrims were blessed in their church, and received their staff

85 The Romanesque west front of St Cuthbert's Cathedral, Durham.

and scrip from the altar. Some took this opportunity to gift land or income to their church. Some returned with relics, real or spurious, one such example being William Preston, who brought back the relic of the arm of St Giles from that saint's shrine near Marseilles, and gifted this to his own church of St Giles in Edinburgh in 1455. The excavation of graves in that church has revealed what appear to be the iron prick ends of two pilgrims' staffs, buried with their owners.

St Cuthbert's shrine at Durham Cathedral

Scots devotion to St Cuthbert was led by royalty; the list of benefactors displayed in the great cathedral started with Edgar (1097–1107) who was regarded as one of the founders. Edgar's brother Alexander was present at the translation of the relics in 1104, and his younger brother David I also supported the building works (85). A visit David made to the shrine illustrates the prohibition of women devotees. A woman servant in his party disguised herself as

a man to gain entry to the feretory, but was struck down by heavenly intervention as she passed the stone in the church which marked the limit of the area accessible to women. A description of the shrine survives from late medieval times: there was a marble and gold sarcophagus which was usually hidden beneath a locked, but removable painted and gilded wooden cover. On feast days the cathedral officials would lift the cover by pulling on ropes linked to pulleys under the vault. Little bells were fixed to the ropes '...so as when the cover was drawn up the bells did make such a good sound it did stir all the peoples hearts that was within the church to repair unto it to make their prayers to God and holy St Cuthbert, and yet the beholders might see the glorious ornaments thereof'. The same account describes the rich decorations on the walls of the feretory chapel, along with relic cupboards which were opened when the shrine was revealed. From the mid fourteenth century on, Scots pilgrims would have been galled to see one of their great national relics, the Black Rood, proudly displayed in the south choir aisle. This was a beautiful reliquary for a fragment of the True

Cross which was brought to Scotland by St Margaret, and removed from Scotland by Edward I in 1296, along with the Stone of Destiny. The Black Rood was returned by Edward III after the English agreed to come to terms with the Scots, the treaty being conditional on the return of various national treasures and documents, including the Coronation Stone. The latter part of the bargain was not honoured, and was overlooked by the Scots, possibly because this was overshadowed by their delight in the repossession of the Black Rood, indicating the very high level of devotion attached to this relic. The Scot's pleasure was short-lived; this powerful relic was recaptured along with David II (1329–71) at the Battle of Neville's Cross in 1346.

Walsingham and Canterbury

The priory at Walsingham in Norfolk became a famed place of pilgrimage after Henry III, in 1223, expressed his personal devotion to the miracle-working statue of the Virgin that was enshrined here. This was kept in a Lady Chapel known as the Holy House, which was built in imitation of the house at Nazareth where the Annunciation took place. The cult was popular with Scots, and evidence of one of the many pilgrimages to this shrine was found during the excavations on the High Street in Perth. One of the townsfolk, probably in the 1230s or 1240s, had returned with a small tin flask, known as an *ampulla*, which they would have filled with holy water from the healing spring at the shrine. The flask had then been lost or discarded. The ampulla was cast with an image of a church on both sides, which frames the Virgin and Child enthroned on one side, and the Coronation of the Virgin on the other (**89a**).

We have already touched on the special devotion of the Scots to St Thomas Becket (see page 00). This devotion lasted throughout the medieval period, although the practicalities of visiting Canterbury would have depended on the changing state of relations between the two countries (**86**). Ships travelled direct from the east coast ports to Kent, possibly avoiding the need to obtain a safe conduct. The same excavations in Perth produced two Becket ampullae of uncertain date (**89b**). Alexander III (1249–86) travelled to Canterbury on pilgrimage sometime before 1272. The release of David II from captivity in 1357 eased the movement of pilgrims to Canterbury, as represented in the great number of safe conducts that were issued by the English King. On one day alone in April 1363, passes were issued to seven lordly Scots, with entourages totalling 42 individuals.

The clergy who administered shrines kept a careful, authenticated record of healing miracles, so that if needs be they could prove the effectiveness of their saint's intercession. The only miracle certificate to survive from Scotland

86 The crossing of Christ Church Cathedral, Canterbury, seen from the cloister.

ST·WILLIAM·OF·PERTH –
FROM·A·MURAL·PAINTING·IN·FRINDSBURY·CHURCH·KENT·

J·S·RICHARDSON·
– APRIL·06 –

87 St William of Perth, wearing characteristic pilgrims'
garb, including a wide-brimmed hat, a leather satchel, a
staff (possibly with a Santiago scallop top), and a water-
bottle. In Frindsbury Church, Kent, close to his shrine at
Rochester.

was issued at Becket's shrine in 1445, to
Alexander, son of Stephen, a young man from
Aberdeen. He had suffered with crippled feet
from birth, and having failed to be cured at
local shrines, had travelled by ship to Kent,
arriving at the shrine on his knees. His prayers
to the blessed Thomas were answered and
immediately 'restored to the said Alexander the
foundations and soles of his feet'.

St William of Perth – a forgotten Scots saint of Kent

An early sixteenth-century English account tells
of a pious man from Perth, a baker by trade
named William, who set off in the early
thirteenth century on pilgrimage to the Holy
Land (87). He planned to visit St Thomas'
shrine at Canterbury, going via the Cathedral of
St Andrew at Rochester. He was murdered
there, and given burial in the cathedral because
of miracles associated with his corpse. This soon
became a major place of pilgrimage, no doubt
benefiting from such close proximity to
Canterbury. In 1220 the wealth of offerings was
sufficient to fund the rebuilding of the choir at
Rochester. St William was formally canonized in
1256; only a small fragment of his grand shrine
of Purbeck marble now survives. He seems to
have been ignored by the Scots, possibly because
he chose to bless the English with miracles
rather than his own folk, and consequently there
are no dedications to him in Scotland.

Shrines of the Holy Blood, and St John the Baptist

Shrines and cults would sometimes fall in and
out of favour; there was a growth in devotion to
shrines related to the Passion of Christ from the
fourteenth century onwards, and three famous
centres in northern Europe claimed to have
relics of the Holy Blood – Hailes Abbey near
Bristol, Bruges in Flanders, and Wilsnack in
Brandenburg, northern Germany. These were
reasonably accessible to the Scots, especially the
Flanders shrine, as Bruges was Scotland's major
continental trading centre, and the starting-

point for many more distant pilgrimages. They would have felt at home there among the Scots merchant community with their own church. Pilgrimages might involve visits to a number of these shrines, such as that recorded in the safe conducts granted in 1451 to two Scots clerics, James Hunter and Henry Howard. They were fulfilling a vow to visit Wilsnack, Canterbury, Walsingham and Hailes.

There are numerous records showing the popularity amongst Scots of the shrine of St John the Baptist at Amiens in northern France. This cult developed in the early thirteenth century when part of the skull, and the silver dish on which it rested, was brought to Amiens by a crusader who had 'liberated' the relic at the siege of Constantinople. The people of Perth considered themselves to be especially favoured by St John, to whom their burgh church was dedicated. In 1995 Perth Museum came into possession of a thirteenth-century Amiens' badge, which probably represents a souvenir of one of many pilgrimages from St John's *toun* to St John's shrine (**91c**). Indeed more pilgrims' badges have been found in Perth than in any other Scottish burgh, although this is probably only due to the greater intensity of archaeological investigation there. This group includes an eagle badge which may be a memento of St John the Evangelist. A rare example of a personal reliquary of a crucifix, was found on the Tay near Newburgh, south-east of Perth. This was hinged to reveal the space where a small fragment of a miracle-working rood would have been contained (**91f**).

Santiago de Compostela

There was a universal belief that the body of the Apostle James the Greater rested in the Galician shrine, having been miraculously transported there from Jerusalem, following his martyrdom in AD 42. From the eleventh century, pilgrimage to Santiago de Compostela became second only to Rome, and the scallop shell badge of the pilgrimage was becoming one of the most highly recognizable logos of all

time. It seems likely that the success of this badge sparked the other shrines to adopt and manufacture their own insignia. The badge aided the promotion of the cult, which was also supported by excellent promotional literature. There is a tradition that Malcolm IV (1153–65) made the pilgrimage, which would have encouraged its popularity with Scots from an early date. The saint was also embraced by Scots thanks to the personal devotion of the powerful Stewart family, especially once their royal dynasty was established at the end of the fourteenth century.

Although very distant from Scotland, there was an extremely well managed apparatus of travel and accommodation, which helped make the journey achievable. Most Scots *en route* to Santiago would have travelled to the south coast of England to embark on a pilgrims' ferry destined either for Bordeaux, or La Corunna, the port closest to Santiago. The voyage from Plymouth to Santiago could be done in four days. The sea route became more popular following improvements in ship design in the fourteenth century, and the introduction of the 'cog' type of vessel. This had a large hull and floated high in the water, allowing more accommodation. One of these was licensed by the English Crown to carry 160 pilgrims. Those arriving at Bordeaux had a lengthy journey by land ahead of them: 200 km (125 miles) to get to the Pyrenees, and then more than 700 km (435 miles) along the difficult *Camino* which ran the full width of northern Spain, crossing two mountain ranges and an arid plain. At least the pilgrims had the benefit of a remarkable chain of hospices, each a day's walk apart, administered by various monastic and military orders. Many would have timed their journey to be present at the main feast day on 25 July, when additional indulgences were granted over and above the standard remission of one-third of all sins. A plenary indulgence, giving remission from all sin, was granted by the Pope to all attending the Cathedral of Santiago when the feast day fell on a Sunday, as it will in 1999.

115

On arrival at the basilica they were confronted by the magnificent west doorway, the Portico de la Gloria, created 1168–88, where the pilgrimage rituals commenced, just as they do today. Having made their prayers at the shrine, they would have obtained their badges from one of the many licensed stalls at the busy market held daily outside the north door of the basilica. The Archbishops of Santiago had received papal approval of their monopoly on souvenir production, and the sale of badges anywhere else was forbidden on pain of excommunication. These were prized possessions, taken home and believed by many to have protective and therapeutic powers, as well as clearly identifying the wearer as one of the blessed who had completed this long and arduous journey. Burials of Santiago pilgrims, wearing their badges, have been found in excavations in various parts of Europe, including the fourteenth-century example from the Isle of May in Fife (see page 63). The first gilded lead scallop badge from Scotland, also likely to be of fourteenth-century date, was recently found nearby on the mainland at St Monans (**90a**). A Santiago scallop, with holes pierced in it for attachment to a hat or clothing, was found in the excavations at the High Street, Perth(**90b**). Analysis of a jet bead, found in the excavations at Elcho Nunnery, Perthshire, has revealed that it was made from Galician jet, and therefore was probably part of a rosary obtained at Santiago.

The connection between St Andrews and Santiago has already been mentioned (see page 64), and it is not surprising to find that a number of the bishops of St Andrews made the pilgrimage to Galicia. Bishop William de Landallis set off for Santiago in 1361 with 20 mounted companions. Even though the shrine of their brother apostle attracted far greater volumes of pilgrims, the Bishops could at least take some solace in the knowledge that their own great church of St Andrews was larger than their rival's. The Santiago pilgrimage, having become almost extinct in the nineteenth century, has now regained its popularity throughout Europe, receiving hundreds of thousands of pilgrims each year.

Rome

As elsewhere in Europe, the Scots looked to Rome as the centre of the Church, and as a place invested with special prestige and holy power, much of which stemmed from the extraordinary collection of relics housed in St Peter's and in many other churches. The greatest shrines were the tombs of St Peter and St Paul beneath the high altar in St Peter's, the former being the father of the Church and thereby the keeper of the keys to the gates of heaven. But there was a plethora of other relics, including: the ark of the covenant, the tablets of Moses, the tunic of the Virgin, loaves and fishes which fed the 5000, and the table used at the Last Supper. The greatest number of Scots who experienced Rome were clerics and not pilgrims as such, there as litigants and supplicants to the Papal Court. King Macbeth made a pilgrimage to Rome in 1050, which is both one of the oldest on record, and the only known royal pilgrimage to the eternal city. A St Peter's pilgrims' badge was found at Whithorn, and another, probably fourteenth-century in date, has been found in the excavations at Finlaggan, the capital of the MacDonald Lords of the Isles (**91d**).

Scots could gain passage on one of the many merchant ships travelling to Bruges from the east coast burgh ports. The most popular time to depart would have been in early spring, planning to arrive in Rome in time for the ceremonies of Holy Week and Easter. The numbers probably declined during the thirteenth century due to wars in Italy, but this might have been reversed by the Jubilee Year pilgrimage of 1300 instituted by the Pope, with special indulgences attached. A Jubilee was created at the beginning of each century, and subsequently at other times. Huge numbers were attracted from throughout Christendom, with two priests on duty day and night at the Basilica of St Peter, gathering up the money offerings with rakes. The Jubilee of 1450 attracted many Scots, including a very large party led by William, Earl of Douglas, together with the Bishop of St Andrews and other great lords, knights and gentlemen, plus 80 attendants. Arrangements would have been made in advance for them to be accommodated in some suitably grand style, with an official welcome from a senior Papal dignitary. In the same year, less well-off Scots could have found a bed, along with the company of their own kind, in the newly created national hospice of Santa Andrea delle Fratte (88). This old church and convent was probably acquired and converted into a hospice with funds provided by the creation of a confraternity in Scotland. The hospice would have provided lodgings, alms, medicine, and burial, as required. A panoramic plan of Rome in 1606 shows the hospice located on the outskirts of the city, close to the Pincian Hill. Pilgrims would have included the wonders of Rome in their sightseeing itinerary; one group visited the San Callisto catacombs on the Via

Appia, and left behind graffito on the walls which read – 'some Scots have been here', accompanied by the date 1467.

Jerusalem and the Holy Land

Some of the Scots in Rome were *en route* to the Holy Land, the longest and most dangerous pilgrimage possible, which usually entailed hundreds of miles on bad roads, and weeks in a small boat. Safe conducts for this journey were often for periods of two or three years. The careful and well-organized pilgrim would have spent Easter in Rome, and then travelled on to Venice for the great festival of St Mark on 25 April, before booking passage for Jaffa, the port for Jerusalem. The Holy Land offered the greatest spiritual rewards of all, with pilgrims being cleansed of all sins as they entered the Holy Sepulchre, built over Christ's tomb. They would also visit as many of the other holy places

88 The Scots hospice in Rome, Santa Andrea delle Fratte, is shown at the centre of this extract from a panoramic plan dated 1606.

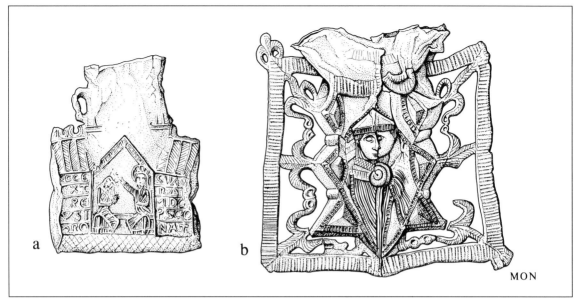

89 *Ampullae* and badges brought back by returning pilgrims: a. *Ampulla* from Walsingham b. *Ampulla* from Canterbury (Actual size. Drawn by Marion O'Neil.)

as possible, in Jerusalem, Nazareth, Bethlehem, at the River Jordan, and the tomb of St Catherine. The numbers visiting Jerusalem, when travel was possible, were enormous. The infrastructure was equally impressive, and one hospice was reputed to have 2000 beds.

Rognvald, Earl (and later saint) of Orkney, accompanied by Bishop William, set off on a two-year pilgrimage to the Holy Land in 1151.

Their departure is recorded in the great Maes Howe chambered tomb, where some of their party scratched a runic inscription while waiting for fair weather. They travelled via Spain, getting up to some traditional Viking exploits on the way. They visited the holy places, and swam in the Jordan, before sailing from Acre to Constantinople, and then on to southern Italy. They followed the Scandinavian pilgrimage

90 a. Scallop shell from Santiago found in Perth, b. Gilded lead scallop badge c 1300 from Santiago found near St Monans (Actual size. Drawn by Marion O'Neil.)

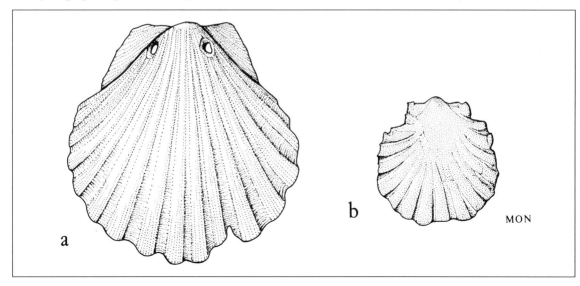

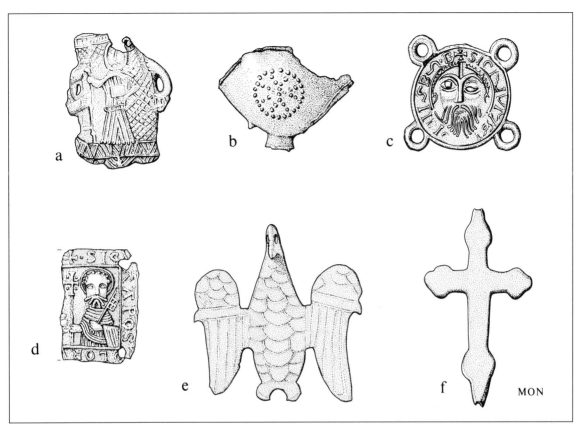

91 *Ampullae* and badges brought back by returning pilgrims: a. *Ampulla* from unidentified source found in Craigmillar (Edinburgh) b.*Ampulla* from unidentified source found in Haddington c. Badge of St John the Baptist from Amiens found in Perth d. Badge from St Peter's, Rome found at Finlaggan, Islay e. Eagle badge (St John the Evangelist?) found in Perth f. Personal crucifix reliquary found in Perth (Actual size. Drawn by Marion O'Neil.)

route north to Denmark, and Norway, arriving home in time for Christmas 1153.

King Robert I (1306–29) had commanded his friend Sir James Douglas '...to send the heart instead of the body, to acquit myself of my vow ... carry my heart to the Holy Sepulchre, where our lord was buried'. A safe conduct of seven years' duration was issued by Edward III, and in spring 1330 the party of knights and men-at-arms set off from Berwick. This was to be a crusade and a pilgrimage 'to fight for the Cross in reclaiming the holy places'. They sailed to the south of Spain and joined with the King of Castile in fighting the Saracens, where Sir James was killed. The heart was then returned for burial at Melrose. This expedition was successful, however, in that credibility was restored to the Scottish cause in the eyes of the papacy, resulting in the removal of the excommunication applied during the excesses of the Wars of Independence. James I (1406–37) achieved a more successful posthumous pilgrimage; following his murder, his heart was

entrusted to Sir Alexander Seton whose journey via Bruges, Basle, Venice and Rhodes can be charted by the financial arrangements he made at these places for the return journey. He presented his King's heart at the Holy Sepulchre, but then died at Rhodes, although the heart was returned safely for burial at the Charterhouse in Perth.

During the crusades from the twelfth century on, Military Orders were established, such as the Knights Hospitallers who served to protect pilgrims in Palestine. These Orders were supported by substantial lands and rents in

92   The annual pilgrimage from Whitekirk to St Mary's, Haddington, in East Lothian.

Scotland. The maintenance of the holy places was also achieved at a great distance, with confraternities of the shrines being established, and altars dedicated to these cults set up in Scottish churches, collecting alms. Many of these were dedicated to the holy virgin martyr, St Catherine, whose shrine in the Sinai desert was held to be the most remote in Christendom. A stone from her tomb, set in a silver reliquary, was listed in the 1432 Inventory of Glasgow Cathedral. Numerous such relics were obtained by pilgrims, causing great damage to the shrines.

Even James III (1460–88), described as 'that most static of kings', seems to have expressed some interest in undertaking this pilgrimage. In 1471 he received a written account of the travels in the Holy Land undertaken by his adviser,

Anselm Adornes, a diplomat and merchant of Bruges. Adornes may have been on reconnaissance for the Duke of Burgundy in advance of a crusade, the dream of which died with the Duke in 1477. This account would have been familiar to James IV (1488–1513), and may have provided some of the inspiration for a pilgrimage and a crusade, which never came to fruition (see page 105). The pilgrimage undertaken by Archbishop Robert Blacader of Glasgow in 1508 is generally seen as being a preparatory trip for his King. Blacader travelled to Rome for Easter, and then on to Venice, where he was received with great honour by the Doge. Rather than hiring the state galley, he chose a cheaper vessel, of a type renowned for their cramped, unsanitary conditions – a decision he did not live to regret. Sadly the Archbishop and most of his large retinue died during the voyage. (92)

Pilgrimage places to visit

HS indicates a property in the care of Historic Scotland

Birsay, Orkney Christchurch (Parish Church of St Magnus)
In the centre of the village, just south of the Earl's Palace. The key is available at the village shop. First place of burial and enshrinement of St Magnus in 1117.

Dunfermline, Fife, Abbey of St Margaret and the Holy Trinity (HS)
The first Benedictine monastery in Scotland was established at the royal chapel in Dunfermline, at the request of Queen Margaret, some time before 1089. Outlines of the early churches of the eleventh and twelfth centuries can be seen within the floor of the nave. The nave, strongly influenced by the architecture of Durham, is in the care of Historic Scotland, as is the adjacent palace. The heavily rebuilt choir is still used for worship; a display of the relics and tomb of King Robert I can be seen here. The remains of the shrine chapel of St Margaret are located to the east of the choir, and are accessible at all times.

Dunkeld, Perth and Kinross, Cathedral of St Columba (HS)
The choir remains in use, while the rest is cared for by Historic Scotland. The early sculpted stones can be seen in the chapter house off the choir.

Edinburgh, St Triduana's Chapel (HS)
In the Restalrig area, 3 km (2 miles) to the east of central Edinburgh. The key for the chapel is available from the shop near the entrance to the kirkyard, during normal opening hours.

Egilsay, Orkney St Magnus' Church (HS)
Earl Magnus was murdered here in 1117, just to the south-east of the church. The site is marked by a monument. This church, with its striking round tower, was probably started in about 1137, the same year as the cathedral at Kirkwall. There is a daily ferry from Tingwall on the north side of the Orkney mainland.

Eileach an Naoimh, Argyll (HS)
An early Christian monastery on an uninhabited island, possibly founded by St Brendan who died in 577. The monastery may have come under the influence of Iona, and is sometimes associated with the documented daughter house known as Ailech. The main enclosure, which includes an underground cell, is dominated by later medieval buildings. A double beehive cell of early Irish type can be seen close to the landing, and an early graveyard overlooks the site from the south. Boat trips can be arranged from Ardfern (telephone 01852 500616).

Glasgow, Cathedral of St Kentigern (HS)
At the north end of the High Street, to the east of the modern city centre. The laigh church (crypt) contains the vaulted tomb of the saint. The well and possible shrine fragments are in the south-east corner of the crypt. This is the most complete large reliquary church in central

Scotland, with much of it dating from the thirteenth century.

Glendochart, Stirlingshire, Priory of St Fillan
The site of the small Augustinian monastery, founded by King Robert I in 1317, is on the West Highland Way between Crianlarich and Tyndrum, just off the A82. St Fillan's Pool is in the River Fillan, just to the north-west of the ruined church.

Govan Old Parish Church, Glasgow
In the centre of Govan next to the Pearce Institute. An important collection of early Christian sculpted stones dating from the ninth to the twelfth century, including the so-called sarcophagus of St Constantine.

Inchcolm, Fife, Priory of St Columba (HS)
The best preserved small monastery in Scotland, and later medieval cult centre of St Columba. Boats from Hawes Pier, South Queensferry.

Inchinnan New Parish Church, Renfrewshire
A group of early Christian stones including a shrine or sarcophagus cover, c 900. Side road off the A8 to Inchinnan village. The stones are in a covered area between the church and the bell-tower.

Iona, Argyll, Abbey of St Mary
Located off the west of Mull. The thirteenth-century Benedictine church and claustral ranges have been heavily rebuilt or restored. St Columba's shrine, Tòrr an Aba, and the high crosses are all located to the west of the church. The Street of the Dead leads the visitor from the village to the abbey, past the nunnery and the medieval parish church of St Ronan, and past St Oran's chapel and burial-ground.

Isle of May, Fife, Priory of St Ethernan
Excavated remains of early Christian chapels and a twelfth-century Cluniac monastery, located within a National Nature Reserve in the care of Scottish Natural Heritage. Daily boat

trips from Anstruther, May–September (telephone 01333 310103).

Kirkwall, Orkney, Cathedral of St Magnus
A reliquary church built to house the bones of the martyred Earl. Largely built in the twelfth to the thirteenth century, exhibiting the influence of Durham Cathedral in the architecture. Artefacts associated with the cult are displayed in Tankerness House Museum opposite the cathedral.

Melrose, Roxburghshire, Abbey of St Mary (HS)
Cult centre of St Waltheof and burial-place of the heart of King Robert I. The tomb-shrine remains are displayed in the Commendator's House museum within the abbey. This is the starting point for the St Cuthbert's Way, a long-distance footpath which runs from here to Lindisfarne.

Melrose, Old Melrose, Ettrick and Lauderdale
The site of St Aidan's monastery founded in the seventh century on the banks of the Tweed, where St Cuthbert entered religion. This can be seen best from Scott's View on the B6356 to the east of Melrose.

Musselburgh, East Lothian, Chapel of Loretto
The possible remains of the chapel, later re-used as an ice-house, can be seen near the entrance to Loretto School.

Papa Westray, Orkney, St Boniface and St Tredwell
The island can be reached by sea or by air from Kirkwall; it takes about 30 minutes to walk between the two pilgrimage places. On the west shore of the island is the early Christian site of St Boniface's, now occupied by a twelfth-century church. The rich remains of a multi-period settlement can be seen eroding out of the cliff just to the west of the church. The overgrown remains of the chapel of St Tredwell can be seen on a promontory projecting into the loch which has taken her name.

Paisley, Abbey of St Miren
The foremost Scottish Cluniac abbey, founded in 1160. Medieval nave with heavily restored transepts, and reconstructed choir. The chapel of St Miren is located in the south transept where the sculpted panels illustrating the life of the saint can still be seen.

Peebles, Tweeddale, Cross Kirk (HS)
To the north of the centre of Peebles, 10 minutes walk from the High Street. The ruined remains of the thirteenth-century church and later medieval friary of the Trinitarians. The remains of the unusual shrine are incorporated within the south wall of the church.

St Andrews, Fife, Cathedral Priory (HS)
The relic chapel is located at the east end of the ruined cathedral. Nearby are the remains of St Rule's and St Mary's churches. The St Andrews' sarcophagus can be seen in the site museum. The Pends gatehouse, and St Leonard's chapel can be found just to the south-west of the priory. There is an excellent display on pilgrimage within the St Andrews' Museum, in Kinburn House to the west of the town centre.

Tain, Ross and Cromarty, Collegiate Church of St Duthac
The medieval reliquary church of the cult of St Duthac, as patronized by James IV, stands within the kirkyard off Tower Street. A slightly earlier ruined church of thirteenth- to fourteenth-century date stands to the south-east of the collegiate church. The pilgrimage is interpreted at the adjoining Tain Through Time visitor centre. The saint's relics had originally been enshrined in the oldest surviving church, the

ruins of which can be found in the kirkyard by the sea, to the north of the churches in the town.

Whitekirk, East Lothian, St Mary's Church
A medieval parish church in the village of Whitekirk, 5 km (3 miles) south-east of North Berwick. Possible fragments a pilgrims' hostel in the kirkyard, just east of the east end of the church. The site of the famed holy well is in the field 200 m (220 yds) to the east.

Whithorn, Cathedral Priory of St Ninian and St Martin (HS)
Through the gatehouse on the west side of George Street. The ruined priory and undercroft, the remains of various excavated structures, the museum of the early Christian stones, and the Whithorn Dig visitor centre, can all be visited.

Whithorn, St Ninian's Chapel, Isle of Whithorn (HS)
Park in the village 5 km (3 miles) south-east of Whithorn, where there is a signposted footpath from the south end of village to the headland. The thirteenth-/fourteenth-century chapel served the resident community, as well as pilgrims landing at the harbour from Ireland and the Isle of Man.

Whithorn, St Ninian's Cave (HS)
Park at Kidsdale, 5 km (3 miles) south-west of Whithorn. A 1.8 km (1 mile) walk down the glen to a stony beach; the cave is to the west. Long regarded as a devotional retreat used by St Ninian. Numerous early sculpted stones were found here in the nineteenth century. These are now in the museum at the priory. There is evidence of continuing devotion with crosses and graffiti of various times up to the present day.

Further reading

* indicates other books in the Historic Scotland/Batsford series.

Bourke, C. (ed) *Studies in the Cult of St Columba*, Dublin, 1997.

Crawford, B. (ed) *St Magnus Cathedral and Orkney's Twelfth Century Renaissance*, Aberdeen, 1988.

Cruden, S. *Scottish Medieval Churches*, Edinburgh, 1986 .

Fawcett, R. *Scottish Abbeys and Priories*, London, 1994.*

Fawcett, R. *Scottish Cathedrals*, London, 1997.*

Finucane, R. *Miracles and Pilgrims: popular beliefs in medieval England*, London, 1995.

Foster, S. *Picts, Gaels and Scots*, London, 1996.*

Hall, U. *St Andrew and Scotland*, St Andrews, 1994.

Harbison, P. *Pilgrimage in Ireland*, London, 1991.

Hill, P. *Whithorn and St Ninian*, Stroud, 1997.

Lynch, M. *Scotland A New History*, London, 1991.

McRoberts, D. (ed) *The Medieval Church of St Andrews*, Glasgow, 1976.

MacQuarrie, A. *The Saints of Scotland*, Edinburgh, 1997.

Marsden, J. *The Illustrated Life of St Columba*, Edinburgh, 1995.

National Museums of Scotland. *Angels, Nobles and Unicorns: art and patronage in medieval Scotland*, Edinburgh, 1982.

Palsson, H. and Edwards, P. *Orkneyinga Saga*, London, 1978.

Ritchie, A. *Iona*, London, 1997.*

Royal Commission on the Ancient and Historical Monuments of Scotland. *Argyll Inventory*, volume 4, *Iona*, Edinburgh, 1982.

Sharp, M. *Holy Places of Celtic Britain*, London, 1997.

Sumption, J. *Pilgrimage, an image of medieval religion*, London, 1975.

Towill, E. *The Saints of Scotland*, Edinburgh, 1983.

Wilson, A. *St Margaret Queen of Scotland*, Edinburgh, 1993.

Yeoman, P. *Medieval Scotland*, London, 1996.*

Index

Page references in **bold** indicate illustrations and plates

Aberdeen 103, 106, 107, 114
Aberdeen Martyrology and Breviary (Bishop Elphinstone) 15, 32, 44
Abernethy, religious centre 53
Abernethy, John 50
Acca of Hexham, Bishop 53
accommodation 13, 38, 111
  Inverkeithing 59
  St Andrews 55
  Santiago de Compostela 115
  Scotlandwell 58
  see also hospitals
Acre 118
Adomnán, Abbot of Iona (later Saint) 80, 111
  Vita Columbae 63, 75-6, 77
Adrian (Ethernan), Saint **62**, 63, 64, 103, 106
Aidan, Saint 45, 122
Alba, kingdom of 14
Alexander III, King 48, 72, 107, 113
Alexander III, Pope 19
Alexander (later King Alexander I) 55, 112
Alexander, son of Stephen 114
Amiens, France 115, **119**
ampullae 27, 113, **118, 119**
Andrew, Saint 14, 44, 53, 54, 55
  oak statue of **68**
  sarcophagus at St Andrews 54, **54**, 123
Anglian kingdom of Northumbria 36
Angus I, King 53
Annales Cambriae 16
Annals of Ulster 106
Annandale 16
Anselm Adornes 120
Ansthruther, Fife 106, 122
Apostles Stone, Dunkeld 86, **86**
Arbroath 89, 90, 106
Arbroath Abbey 19, 90
Arcluf, Gaulish bishop 111
Ardersier 103
Argyll 75
  Eileach an Naoimh 121
  see also Dál Riata
Armagh 106
Atholl 90
Augustinians
  at St Andrews 55
  at Scone 64
  nuns at Iona 81
  St Fillan's Priory 91, 122
Auldhame, church at 50
Awlson, Walter 74

Baldred, Saint 49-50, **50**
Bangor, Co. Down 30

Bannockburn, Battle of 55, 67, 89, 90-1
Bass Rock, St Baldred's chapel 50, **50**
Bay of the Martyrs, Iona 79
Beaton, Archbishop James 27
Becket, Saint Thomas 18, 19, 20-1, 27, 58, 90, 95, 113-14
Bede 33, 36
bell-shrines 87, 106
  Guthrie bell-shrine 87, **88**
  Kilmichael Glassary 87, **87**
Benedictine Order
  Dunfermline 71, 121
  Iona 79, 81-2, 122
  Isle of May 63
Bernard, Abbot 90
Bernard, Saint 19
Berwick 109, 119
Bethlehem 118
Birsay, Orkney 94-5, 96, 97, 121
Blacader Aisle, Glasgow Cathedral 16, **17, 24**, 27
Blacader, Archbishop Robert 105, 120
Black Cart, River 29
Black Rood 112-13
Bladnoch, River 37
Blathmac (monk) 80
Blebo 59
Boardhouse Mill, Orkney 96
Boece, Hector (chronicler) 29
Bondington, Bishop William 19, 20-1
Bonduff of Dunkirk, William 69
Book of Kells 79
Bordeaux 115
Bothwell Castle 105
Bourke, Cormac 87
Bower, Walter 64, 90
Breac Beannach see Monymusk Reliquary
Brendan, Saint 121
broch, Papa Westray 99
Brooke, Daphne, historian 13
Brough of Birsay, Orkney 94, 95
Brough of Deerness, Orkney 100
Brown, Peter, historian 11
Brown, William (pilgrim) 110
Bruce, Marjorie **31**
Bruce, Robert the *see* Robert I, King
Bruges, Flanders 31, 114-15, 116, 119, 120
Bury St Edmunds, Abbot of 110

Caithness 96
Camino, Spain 115
Candida Casa, Whithorn 33, 37
Canterbury
  ampulla from **118**

Christ Church Cathedral 19, 20, 21, 71, **113**, 114, 115
Carlisle 33
Cathach of St Columba 87-8, **89**
Celtic Church 99
Ceres 59
Chalmers, Peter MacGregor 82, **83**
Christchurch, Birsay 94, 95, 121
cist, Bronze Age, at Peebles 48
cist-cemeteries, Isle of May 63
Cistercians
  at Melrose Abbey 45, 46, 50
  nuns at North Berwick 59
  and Whitekirk shrine 50, 51
cistern, stone-lined: St Kentigern's tomb 27
Cladh an Disirt, Iona 79, 81
Clairvaux 19
Clonmacnoise, Ireland 79
Cluniac Order 30, 122, 123
Clyde, River 18, 29
Cnoc an t-Sithein, Iona (Hill of the Angels) 76
Coble Point, River Eden 58
Colmcille's Well 79
Columba, Saint 11, 21, 35, 36, 55, 63, 75-80
  cult of 81-5, 122
  and Dunkeld 80, 85-7, **86**, 89
  relics 54, 64, 76, 79-80, 85-90, **86, 89, 91**
  rule of 75, 80
Conall mac Comgaill, High King 75
Congal, Saint 30
Constantine of Govan, Saint 18, 28-9, **28**, 122
Constantine, King, son of Fergus 54
Constantinople 115, 118
Conval, Saint 29
Corbridge, Battle of 86
'Cradle of the north wind', Iona Abbey 81, **81**
Craigmillar, Edinburgh, *ampulla* **119**
Crail, Fife 103, 106
crannog, Papa Westray 99
Crawford, James 32
Cromarty 103
Crossgates 58
Crossraguel 103
crusades 27, 46, 49, 105, 119, 120
Crustan, Orkney 96
Culdees (monks) 55
Culross, Fife, St Serf's monastery 16
cults
  influence on building 16
  Loretto 51
  of Pictish saints 99
  promotion of 14-15

renewal of interest in 69
  of St Andrew 53, 55
  of St Columba 81-5
  of St Kentigern 18-22, 27-8
  of St Margaret 74
  of St Miren 30
  of St Ninian 33, 36, 42-4
  of St Waltheof 18
Cumbria 18
Cupar 57
curraghs 36, 79
Cuthbert, Saint 21, 45, 46, 96, 109, 112-13

Dairsie Castle 57
Dál Riata 75, 90
Darnaway Castle 105
David de Bernham, Bishop 72
David I, King 29, 30, 63, 110
  church at Dunfermline 71, **71**
  and Durham Cathedral 112
  and Melrose Abbey 45
  and St Kentigern's cult 18, 28
  tomb in Dunfermline Abbey 73
David II, King 113
Dominic, Abbot of Iona 84
Donald, Lord of the Isles 85
Douai, France, Scots seminary 42, 73
Douglas, Sir James 119
drove-roads 91
Druids 35
Dumbarton, royal centre 29
Dumfries, religious houses in 38
Dunbar 51, 60
Duncan, Professor Archie 13
Duncan, Earl 59
Duncan, King 80
Dundee 32, 58
Dundrennan Abbey 38, **48**
Dunfermline 79
  masons from 96
  and Queen Margaret 71-4
Dunfermline Abbey Church **70**, 71-3, **71, 72, 73, 74**, 121
  well 65
Dunkeld 53, 64
  Columban relics 80, 85-7, **86**, 89
  Dunkeld Cathedral 86, **86**, 87, 121
  Chapter Seal 86-7, **86**
Dupplin Cross, Constantine 29
Durham, masons from 96
Durham Cathedral 71, 96, 112-13, **112**, 121, 122
Duthac, Saint 14, 101, 103, 105, 106-9, **107-8**, 123

Earlsferry, by Elie 59, 62
Earlsferry hospital 60-2
Earn, River 57
Eden, River 57, 58

Edgar, King 112
Edinburgh 51, 58, 101, 103, 106, 107, 111
    Craigmillar **119**
    St Mary's RC Cathedral Church 70-1
    St Triduana's well-shrine of Restalrig 51-2, **52**, 121
Edward the Confessor, tomb of **14**
Edward I, King 21, 28, 62, 113
Edward II, King 42
Edward III, King 51, 113, 119
Egilsay island 94, 95, 96, 97, **98**, 121
Elcho Nunnery, Perthshire, jet bead 116
Elgin 103, 105, 106
Elie 59, 62
Elphinstone, Bishop William, *Aberdeen Breviary* 15, 32
Enoch *see* Thenew, Saint
Eshiels, near Peebles 49
Ethernan (later Adrian), Saint **62**, 63, 64, 103, 106
Evie, Orkney 96
ex-votos **23**, 26
Eynhallow, Orkney 96

Fast Castle, Berwickshire **48**, 51
feast days/festivals
    James IV's pilgrimages 101
    significance of 14
    Durham Cathedral 112
    Iona 84
    Peebles 49
    St Andrews 65, 67
    St Baldred 50
    St Columba 64
    St Conval 29
    St Fillan 91
    St Kentigern **23**, 24
    St Magnus' Cathedral, Kirkwall 97
    St Margaret, at Dunfermline 72, 73, 74
    St Miren 30
    Santiago de Compostela 115
    Whithorn 39
Fergus of Galloway 36
Fergus (holy man) 16
Fergus, King 54
Fergus, Saint 16
Fife, Earls of 57, 59
Fillan, River 91, 122
Fillan, Saint 90-2, **91**, 122
Finlaggan, Islay, pilgrim's badge 116, **119**
Finnian, Saint 35-6, 39
Fisher, Ian 79
Flemish *Book of Hours* 106
Flodden, Battle of 109
Foodieash 57
Fordun (chronicler) 46, 48-9
Forgan, old parish church at 58
Forth, Firth of 54, 55, 58, 59, 60-4, **62**
Fortrose 106
Fothad 54
Franciscan friary, Inverkeithing 59
French Revolution 42
Frindsbury Church, Kent **114**

Gaels from Ireland 85
Galbraith, Elizabeth 32
Galloway
    and Anglian kingdom of Northumbria 36
    centre for pilgrims 37-8
    cult of St Ninian 14
    independence of 44
Gallows Hill 57
Giles, Saint **91**, 112
Glasgow 79, 84, 103
    medieval period 16, 26, **26**

seal from 72
Glasgow Airport 29
Glasgow Cathedral 14, 16-28, **17**, 20-2, **24**-6, 28, 32, 46, 111, 120, 121-2
    Chapter Seal 21, **21**
    well 65
Glencolmcille, Donegal 77, 79, 80
Glendalough, Ireland 79
Glendochart and St Fillan 90-2, 122
Glenluce Abbey 38, 103, **104**
Gloucester Cathedral 19
Govan, St Constantine of 18, 28-9, **28**, 122
Greyfriars monastery, Stirling 101
Gryfe, River 29
Guardbridge 58, **59**
Guthrie bell-shrine 87, **88**

Haddington 107, **119**, **120**
Hailes Abbey, Bristol 114, 115
Hakon, Earl 94-5
Haldenstone, Prior James 67, 106
Halidon Hill, Battle of 109
Harris, St Clement's Church, Rodel 85, **85**
healing
    miracle of 14
    St Conval's Chariot 29
    St Fillan's relics 92
    St Kentigern's tomb 24, 27
    St Ninian's cult 39, 42-4
    St Thomas Becket's shrine 114
    St Triduana and eye complaints 52
    St Waltheof 46
    and Whitekirk shrine 51
Hebrides 111
'heid' pilgrimages 32
Henry III, King 113
Henry of St Andrews, Prior 57
Herbert, Bishop 18, 24
Hill of the Angels, Iona 76
Holy Blood, shrines of 114-15
Holy Land
    crusades to 27, 49
    pilgrimages to 95, 105, 110, 111, 114, 117-20
Holy Trinity Church, St Andrews 55
Holyrood Abbey, Edinburgh 107
hospitals
    Earlsferry 60-2
    Loch Leven 58
    St George's, Dunkeld 87
    St Leonard's, Peebles 49
    St Leonard's, St Andrews 55, 64, 69, **69**
    St Mary's, Winchester **56**
    St Nicholas', Glasgow **26**
    St Nicholas', St Andrews 64
    Santa Andrea delle Fratte, Rome 117, **117**
Howard, Henry 115
Hunter, James 115

Inchaffray 91
Inchcolm, Fife 64, 85, 122
Inchinnan 29, 122
Inchkeith, island of 63
indulgences 13, 15, 37, 39, 110, 111
    Glasgow 24
    Holy Well of Our Lady, Whitekirk 51
    Iona pilgrims 84
    Melrose Abbey 45
    Rome pilgrims 116
    St Andrews 65
    St Margaret's feast day, Dunfermline 74
    Santiago de Compostela 115
Innocent III, Pope 52

Innocent IV, Pope 72
Inverkeithing 58, 59
Inverness 105, 106
Iona 14, 21, 75-85, **76**, 77, 87, 106, 121
    monastery 75-7, **77**, 80
    monks of 45, 63, 64
    style of monasticism 35
Iona Abbey 76, **78**, 81, **81**-4, 82-4, 122
Ireland 106
    pilgrims from 37, 39, 85, 123
Iron Age 99
Isle of Man, pilgrims from 38, 39, 123

Jaffa 117
James the Greater of Compostela, Saint 30, 53, 106, 115-16
James I, King 38, 51, 119
James II, King 107
James III, King 49, 52, 105, 120
James IV, King 42, 120
    and Glasgow Cathedral 28
    and Paisley Abbey 31
    pilgrimages
        Cross Kirk, Peebles 49
        Glendochart 92
        Isle of May 64, 101, 103, 106
        Tain 101, 102, 103, 106-9, **108**, 123
        Whitekirk shrine 51
        Whithorn 38, 39, **44**, 101-5
James V, King 49, 51, 106
    infant son of James IV 101
Jerusalem 105, 115, 117-18, 119
jet bead, Elcho Nunnery, Perthshire 116
Jocelin, Bishop of Glasgow 18, 19, 24, 46
Jocelin of Furness, *Life of Kentigern* 18, 24
John, monk of Melrose Abbey 45
John the Baptist, Saint: shrines 115
Johnson, Dr Samuel 75
Jordan, River 118
Julius II, Pope 105

Kells, Co. Meath 80
Kennedy, Janet 105
Kenneth, son of Alpin 80, 85
Kennoway 59
Kentigern, Saint 11, 16-24, 29, 121
    cult of 18-22, 27-8
    shrine 14, 18, 19-20, **20**-3, 21-3, **25**, 27, **28**, 32
Kilmichael Glassary bell-shrine 87, **87**
Kilwinning 103
Kincaple 62
Kinghorn 64
Kinross, pilgrim's badge mould 60, **61**
Kinrymont, St Andrews 53, 55
Kirkcaldy 59
Kirkwall
    St Magnus' Cathedral 93, **93**-8, 95, 96-9, 121, 122
    Tankerness Museum 98, 122
Knights Hospitallers 119
Knights Templars 29

La Corunna 115
Laggangairn standing stones 38
Latinus (stone) 35
Lauder, Bishop William 21, 24
Leith, port of 106
leprosy 44, 59, 64
Leuchars 58
Leven, River 58
Leven valley 59
Lindisfarne 45, 49, 63, 64, 122
Lindisfarne Priory 21

Lindores Abbey 57, **58**
Lindsay, Sir David 51
Links Chapel, Tain 108-9
Linlithgow 106
Linlithgow Palace 51
Lion (warship) 106
Loch Leven 58
Loch Lomond, St Miren 30
Loch Swannay 96
Loch Tay 90
Lochleven Castle 74
Lochore 58
London, pilgrim's badge 60, **61**
Lords of the Isles 18, 81, 85, 87, 103, 116
Loretto chapels 51, 122

Macbeth, King 58, 116
Macdonald Lords of the Isles 103, 116
Macduff's Cross 57
Macleod, Alexander 85, **85**
Madeleine, Princess 51
Madrid, St Margaret's miracles 71
Maes Howe tomb, Orkney 118
Magnus, Earl (Saint) 93-9, **94**, 95, **98**-9, 121, 122
Malcolm Canmore, King 71, 72
Malcolm IV, King 115
Malcolm of Monymusk 90
Manse (Magnus) Well, Orkney 96
Mansie (Magnus) Stones, Orkney 96
Margaret, Countess of Douglas 37
Margaret of Denmark 105
Margaret, Queen (Saint) 54, 55, 58, 80, 105, 113, 121
    canonization 71, 72, 74
    Gospel book 74, **88**
    head shrine of 42, 73, **74**
    shrine 71-3, **72**, 74
Margaret Tudor, Queen 101, 102-3
Margaret (warship) 106
Markinch 59
Marseilles 112
Martin of Tours, Saint 33, 35
Mass Roads, Orkney 95-6, 97, 100
Maxwell, Sir Herbert **43**
May, Isle of **62**, 63-4, **63**, 101, 103, 106, 116, 122
Melrose 32
Melrose Abbey 45-6, **45**, 47, **48**, 119, 122
Melrose Chronicle 46
Melville, Professor James 62
Menai Straits, Battle of 94
Messigate (Mass Road), Papa Westray 100
Milburga, Saint 30
Miracula Niniae Episcopi 36, 39, 42, 44
Miren of Paisley, Saint 30-2, 123
Mochrum, chapel at 39
Molendinar Burn, Glasgow 16, 26
Montrose 106
Monylaw, Thomas 109
Monymusk Reliquary (*Breac Beannach*) 54, 87, 89-90
Moonzie, Holy Trinity parish church 57
Mòr Breac 54
Mull, Island of 75, 79
Musselburgh, Loretto Chapel 51, 122

National Museums of Scotland 46, 87, 89
Nazareth 118
Nechtan, Pictish King 99
Neville's Cross, Battle of 113
Newburgh **58**, 115
Newhaven 106
Nidaros Cathedral, Trondheim, Norway 97

Ninian, Saint 11, 16, 33-44, **34**, **48**, 123
  cult of 14, 33, 36, 42-4
  oak statue 39, **42**
  shrine 33-5, 36, 37, **37**, 39-41, **40**, 101-3, 105
North Berwick 59-60, **60**, **61**
North Queensferry 58
Northside of Birsay 96
Northumbria 36, 53, 99
Northumbrian church, Whithorn 36, **37**

O'Donnell clan 88
Orkney Islands, shrines 52, 93-100, 106, 121, 122
Orkneyinga Saga 93, 94, 95
O'Sullivan, Jerry 77
Outer Hebrides 85, **85**

Paisley 103
Paisley Abbey 29, 30-2, **30-2**, 123
Papa Westray, Orkney 52, 99-100, **100**, 122
Paris, Matthew 74
Partick, royal centre 16, 29
Patras, Greece 53
Patrick, Saint, hand-shrine **91**
Pecthelm, Bishop 33, 36
Peebles, Cross Kirk 46-9, **49**, 123
Pends gatehouse, St Andrews 65, **66**, **69**, 123
Pends Road, St Andrews 53, 64
Penpont 102
Perth 57, **58**, 106, 113, 114
  Charterhouse 119
  Loretto Chapel 51
  pilgrims' badges 60, **61**, 116, **118**, **119**
Peter, Saint, churches dedicated to 36
Physgill Glen 41
Piccolomini (later Pope Pius II) 51
Picts 52, 85, 90
  Columba and 75
  conversion of 33, 63
  craftsmen 89
  and Kenneth, son of Alpin 80
  and Kinrymont, St Andrews 53
  saints' cults 99
'Pilgrim Gait', Pratis 59
pilgrims' badges 38-9, 46, **48**, 60, **61**, 97, **97**, 115, 116, **118**, **119**
Pilgrim's Haven, Isle of May 64
Pitbladdo 57
Pius II, Pope 51
Plymouth 115
Portincrag (Tayport) 58
Pratis 59
Premonstratensian canons, at Whithorn 36, **38**
Preston, William 112
Prestonkirk, church at 50
Provand's Lordship, Glasgow 26
Pyrenees 115

Queen's Ferry 58, 59, 74
Queensferry **57**

Reformation 29, 39, 42, 98, 109
  Dunkeld relics destroyed 87
  St Andrews Cathedral sacked 70
  St Kentigern's tomb destroyed 27
  shrines destroyed 15
  shrines surviving 46
  and Whitekirk shrine 51
Reginald, Lord of the Isles 81
Regulus (St Rule) 51, 53
Reilig Odhráin, Iona 77, 79, 80, 81
relics 11, 13, 14

Cross Kirk, Peebles 49
Glasgow Cathedral 27
Melrose Abbey 46
  of St Andrew 54
  of St Columba 54, 64, 76, 79-80, 85-90, **86**, **89**, **91**
  of St Duthac 107, 108, **108**, 109
  of St Fillan 90-2, **90**
  of St Kentigern 18, 27
  of St Magnus 93, 95-6, **96**, 97-9, **98-9**
  of St Margaret 73-4, **74**
  of St Ninian 35, 42-4
Renfrew 18
Renfrewshire 29, 30
Restalrig, Edinburgh: St Triduana's well-shrine 51-2, **52**, 99, 121
Rhodes 119
Rievaulx, Cistercians of 45
Ritchie, Anna 77, 124
Robert, Bishop 55, 65
Robert of Dunfermline, Abbot 72
Robert I, King **31**, 44, 107
  at St Andrews 55
  at Scotlandwell 58-9
  and Bannockburn 90-1
  heart of 46, 105, 119, 122
  and St Fillan 90-1, 122
  tomb in Dunfermline Abbey 73, 121
Robertson, Niall 92
Rochester, Kent, shrine of St William **114**, **114**
Rognvald, Earl (later Saint) 95, 98, 118
Romanesque style 93, 96, 97, **112**
Rome 36, 53
  pilgrimages to 95, 110, 111, 116-17, **117**, 120
  St Ninian at 33
  St Peter's 19, 39, 116, **119**
Ross: cult of St Duthac 14
Ross, Earls of 103, 107, 109
Ross, Alexander, of Balnagowan 109
Rule, Saint (Regulus) 51, 53

St Andrews 53-62, **66**, 79, 106, 116
  Bishops of 58, 110, 117
  Castle 60
  Cathedral 53, **54**, 64, **65**, 67, **69**, 70, 90, 97, 123
  pilgrimage routes to 55-62, **57**, 64, 72
  pilgrims' badge 60, **61**
  pilgrim's experience 64-70
  and Queen Margaret 54
  university 65, 69
  well 27, 65
'St Baldred's Boat', Seacliff Beach 50
St Baldred's chapel, Bass Rock 50, **50**
St Baldred's Well, Prestonkirk 50
St Boniface Church, Papa Westray 99
St Catherine's monastery, Mount Sinai 111
St Catherine's shrine, Sinai 120
St Clement's Church, Rodel, Harris 85, **85**
St Columba's Bay, Iona 79
St Conval's Chariot 29
St Duthac's Church, Tain 107, 108, 123
St Enoch's Church, Glasgow 26
St Fillan's bell **90**
St Fillan's Priory 91, 92, **92**, 122
'St Finnian's Isle' (Inchinnan) 29

St George's hospital, Dunkeld 87
St Giles' Cathedral, Edinburgh 107, 112
St James' Church, St Andrews 70
St John's Church, Perth 115
St Laurence's shrine, Mearns 71
St Leonard's hospital (hospice), St Andrews 55, 64, 69, **69**
St Leonard's hospitals, Peebles 49
St Machar's Cathedral, Aberdeen 107
St Magnus' Cathedral, Kirkwall 93, **93-8**, 95, 96-9, 121, 122
St Magnus' Church, Egilsay 97, **98**, 121
St Martin's Cross, Iona 77
St Mary's Chapel, Iona 81, 82
St Mary's Church, St Andrews 53, 123
St Mary's RC Cathedral Church, Edinburgh 70-1
St Mary's, Winchester **56**
St Michael's Church, Iona 81
St Miren's Aisle, Paisley Abbey 30-**2**
St Monans, scallop badge 116, **118**
St Nicholas' hospital, Glasgow **26**
St Nicholas' hospital, St Andrews 64
St Ninian's Cave, Whithorn 41-2, **43**, 123
St Olaf's Church, Kirkwall 95
St Ronan's Church, Iona 81, 122
St Rule's Church, St Andrews 54, 55, 123
St Thenew's Well, Glasgow 26
St Tredwell's chapel, Papa Westray 99, 100, **100**, 122
Salisbury 24
Salisbury Book of Hours **34**
San Callisto catacombs, Via Appia 117
Santa Andrea delle Fratte, Rome 117, **117**
Santa Casa (Loretto chapel) 51
Santiago de Compostela 53, 63, **63**, 64, 106, 110, 115-16, **118**
Sarum Ritual 24
scallop shell badges 63, **63**, **114**, 115, 116, **118**
Scandinavia 89, 93-4, 96, 97, 118-19
Scone 16, 32, **58**, 92
Scone Abbey 57, 64
Scotlandwell 57, **57**, 58-9
Scott, Sir Walter 45
Scottish Chronicle 85
Scott's View 45, 122
Seacliff Beach, East Lothian 50
Serf, Saint 16
Seton, Sir Alexander 119
Shaw, Abbot George 31, 32
Shetland 95, 96, 99
signacula (pilgrims' badges) 38-9
Sinai desert, St Catherine's shrine 120
Sinai, Mount, St Catherine's monastery 111
Somerled, Lord of the Isles 18
Spain 118, 119
  see also Santiago de Compostela
Stablegreen Port, Glasgow 26
Stewart, Archbishop Alexander 69
Stewart family 30, 31, 105-6, 115
  royal dynasty 44, 115
Stirling 16, 109
  Greyfriars monastery 101
Stirling Castle 103, 106
Stone of Destiny 113
Stornoway, siege of 103

Strangford, Ulster: monastery at 36
Strathclyde, saints and shrines in 16-32
Strathearn 90
Strathgryfe 29
Strathkinness 57
Street of the Dead, Iona 79, 82, 122
Sweetheart Abbey 42
Symon, Bishop of Galloway 45

Tain, Easter Ross: St Duthac's shrine 101, 103, 105, 106-9, **107-8**, 123
Tankerness Museum, Kirkwall 98, 122
Tay, River 55, 57, 58, 80, 115
Taylor, Dr Simon 55
Tayport 58
Thenew, Saint (Enoch) 16, 26
Thomas, Charles 36
Thomas Tervas of Paisley, Abbot 30-1
Tongland 103
Tòrr an Aba, Iona 77, 82, 122
Tours, St Ninian at 33
trade 13, 33, 35, 62, 114-15
Tredwell, Saint 99, 122
Triduana of Restalrig, Saint 51-2, **52**, 99, 121
Trinitarians 49, **49**, 57, 58, 60, 123
Turgot 45, 58, 71
Tyndrum 90, 122
Tyne, River 50, 51
Tyninghame, monastery at 49-50

Uí Néill royal kin-group 75
Ulster 36
Ulster Museum 87

Venice 117, 119, 120
Via Francigena 110
Vicarsford 58
Vikings 79, 80, 86, 89, 118

Walsingham, Norfolk 113, 115, **118**
Walter Fitz Alan 18, 30
Waltheof, Saint 18, 45-6, **47**, 122
Wardlaw, Bishop 58, 110
Wars of Independence 14, 64, 84, 119
Whitekirk **120**
  Holy Well of Our Lady **48**, 50-1, 123
Whithorn 33-44, **48**, 79, 84, 116
  Candida Casa 33, 37
  cathedral priory 14, 33-41, **37-8**, **40-1**, **43-4**, 44, 123
  and cross find at Peebles 48
  Isle of 39
  James IV visits 38, 39, **44**, 101-5, 106
  well 65
Wigtown 102, 103
Wilfred, Bishop 53
William de Landallis, Bishop of St Andrews 116
William, Earl of Douglas 117
William, Earl of Ross 107
William the Lion, King 19, 71, 89
William of Orkney, Bishop 95, 118
William of Perth, Saint 114, **114**
Wilsnack, Brandenburg, Germany 114, 115
Winchester, St Mary's **56**
Winchester Cathedral 19
Wishart, Bishop Robert 21
Wood, Sir Andrew, of Largo 106
Woodhaven 58
Worcester Cathedral 19

The author
Peter Yeoman has been the Council Archaeologist for Fife since 1989, where his research around St Andrews and on the Isle of May introduced him to the elusive archaeology of pilgrimage. For two years in the late 80s he directed the only major programme of excavations ever to take place in Edinburgh Castle, and is co-author of the monograph entitled *Excavations within Edinburgh Castle* recently published by the Society of Antiquaries of Scotland, of which Peter Yeoman is a Fellow. He is currently Vice President of the Council for Scottish Archaeology.

Series editor: Dr David J. Breeze
Chief Inspector of Ancient Monuments, Historic Scotland

Titles in the series
Periods
Scotland's First Settlers
Caroline Wickham-Jones
Neolithic and Bronze Age Scotland
P.J. Ashmore
Celtic Scotland
Ian Armit
Roman Scotland
David J. Breeze
Picts, Gaels and Scots
Sally Foster
Viking Scotland
Anna Ritchie
Medieval Scotland
Peter Yeoman
Fortress Scotland and the Jacobites
Chris Tabraham and Doreen Grove

Sites and subjects
Ancient Shetland
Val Turner
Edinburgh Castle
Iain MacIvor
Iona
Anna Ritchie
Prehistoric Orkney
Anna Ritchie
Scotland's Castles
Chris Tabraham
Scottish Abbeys and Priories
Richard Fawcett
Stirling Castle
Richard Fawcett
Scottish Cathedrals
Richard Fawcett

Forthcoming
Scotland's Historic Shipwrecks
Colin Martin